United States Government Accountability Office

Reports to the Ranking Member, Committee on Homeland Security and Governmental Affairs, U.S. Senate

July 2013

AGRICULTURAL TRADE

IIIIIIIIIIIIIIIIIIIII
I0448662

USDA Is Monitoring Market Development Programs as Required but Could Improve Analysis of Impact

GAO-13-740

July 2013

GAO Highlights

Highlights of GAO-13-740, a report to the Ranking Member, Committee on Homeland Security and Governmental Affairs, U.S. Senate

AGRICULTURAL TRADE

USDA Is Monitoring Market Development Programs as Required but Could Improve Analysis of Impact

Why GAO Did This Study

USDA administers five programs to assist U.S. agricultural industry efforts to build, maintain, and expand overseas markets. However, members of Congress continue to debate the level of funding for this assistance and its impact on agricultural exports. USDA provides about $250 million annually for the five market development programs. MAP and FMD received about 90 percent of this funding in fiscal year 2012, with allocations of $200 million and $34.5 million, respectively.

GAO was asked to review USDA's market development programs. This report (1) describes participation and expenditures in these market development programs, particularly MAP and FMD; (2) examines FAS's management and monitoring of its market development programs; and (3) assesses FAS's cost-benefit analysis of MAP's and FMD's impact on the U.S. economy. GAO analyzed USDA expenditure data from 2002 through 2011 and reviewed key agency and program participant documents. GAO also assessed a sample of participants' annual progress reports and assessed economic cost-benefit analyses of MAP and FMD commissioned by USDA.

What GAO Recommends

GAO recommends that USDA (1) emphasize that market development program participants' annual progress reports should identify the methodologies used to assess results and (2) ensure that any economic models used in future cost-benefit analyses of the programs include industry-specific variables and sensitivity analyses of key assumptions. USDA concurred with GAO's recommendations.

View GAO-13-740. For more information, contact Lawrance Evans at (202) 512-4802 or evansl@gao.gov.

What GAO Found

Market development program participants use program funds to support a variety of activities intended to raise awareness or acceptance of U.S. agricultural products in overseas markets. Common activities include, among others, market research, consumer and retail promotion, and participation in international trade shows. GAO's analysis of expenditure data from 2007 through 2011 shows that participants in the Market Access Program (MAP) and the Foreign Market Development Program (FMD)—the largest of the five market development programs—remained generally consistent during that period. The program participants with the largest shares of funding and the countries where the largest shares of funds were spent also remained relatively consistent. Expenditure data for 2011 show that MAP and FMD participants met or exceeded FAS contribution requirements that they match minimum percentages of the program funding they receive. Unlike funding for the other programs, a portion of MAP funds is used for promotion of branded products. In 2011, MAP participants spent about 85 percent of program funding on overseas promotion of generic commodities. More than 600 small companies and seven agricultural cooperatives spent the remaining 15 percent of MAP funding to promote branded products.

The U.S. Department of Agriculture's (USDA) Foreign Agricultural Service (FAS) uses several management and monitoring processes to reduce the risk of duplication among the five programs. FAS uses an integrated system to process funding applications for multiple programs and to monitor expenditures, which reduces the risk of duplication. According to FAS officials, FAS also monitors participants' expenses for all programs through its compliance review process. In addition, FAS guidance requires program participants to submit annual progress reports on the results of their market development activities. GAO found that performance measures in a sample of progress reports generally reflected selected FAS guidance and key attributes of successful performance measures that GAO had identified. However, the sampled reports did not always outline the methodologies used to assess activity results as required by FAS guidelines. In these cases, it would be difficult for FAS to determine the reliability of the reported results and the impact of market development activities.

A 2007 cost-benefit analysis of MAP and FMD, commissioned by FAS, found that the programs increased U.S. agricultural exports and benefited the U.S. economy, but methodological limitations may affect the magnitude of the estimated benefits. Overall, the analysis asserted that the government's expenditures for the two programs resulted in greater increases in U.S. agricultural exports and greater benefit to the U.S. economy than would have occurred without the expenditures. However, an economic model used to estimate the programs' impact on U.S. market share omitted important variables, such as commodity prices. Also, the study did not include sensitivity analyses of certain key assumptions underlying its estimates of impacts on U.S. exports. For example, analyses of the possible effects of varying levels of program funding would provide a clearer picture of the potential impact of increased or decreased funding on U.S. exports and the economy. FAS officials reported that they plan to commission a new cost-benefit analysis in 2014 but have not yet identified the methodologies that the new analysis will use.

_____ United States Government Accountability Office

Contents

Tables

Figure

Abbreviations List

EMP	Emerging Markets Program
FAS	Foreign Agricultural Service
FMD	Foreign Market Development Program
MAP	Market Access Program
QSP	Quality Samples Program
TASC	Technical Assistance for Specialty Crops Program
UES	Unified Export Strategy
USDA	United States Department of Agriculture
WUSATA	Western United States Agricultural Trade Association

July 31, 2013

The Honorable Tom Coburn
Ranking Member
Committee on Homeland Security
  and Governmental Affairs
United States Senate

Dear Senator Coburn:

The U.S. Department of Agriculture (USDA) provides about $250 million annually for five market development programs intended to help U.S. agricultural producers increase their exports by building, maintaining, and expanding their overseas markets.[1] In 2010, the administration highlighted the importance of increasing exports, including agricultural exports, when it launched the National Export Initiative with the goal of doubling the dollar value of U.S. exports by 2015. However, members of Congress have debated the level of funding for market development assistance and the impact it has on agricultural exports. The two largest of USDA's five market development programs—the Market Access Program (MAP) and the Foreign Market Development Program (FMD)—received authorizations of, respectively, $200 million and $34.5 million of USDA's annual market development program funding in fiscal year 2012. The three remaining programs' authorizations ranged from $2 million to $10 million in fiscal year 2012. USDA's Foreign Agricultural Service (FAS) administers the five programs. We last reported on MAP in 1999, when we found that USDA's estimate of the program's impact on the U.S. economy may have been overstated and that evidence of the program's impact from available market-level studies was inconclusive.[2] More recently, USDA commissioned a cost-benefit analysis of MAP's and

---

[1] In fiscal year 2012, U.S. agricultural exports totaled $135.8 billion.

[2] GAO, *Agricultural Trade: Changes Made to Market Access Program, but Questions Remain on Economic Impact*, NSIAD-99-38 (Washington, D.C. Apr. 5, 1999).

FMD's economic impact, which was completed in 2007 and updated in 2010.[3]

You asked us to review several aspects of FAS's five market development programs. This report (1) describes participation and expenditures in the programs, particularly MAP and FMD; (2) examines FAS's management and monitoring of its market development programs; and (3) assesses FAS's cost-benefit analysis of MAP's and FMD's impact on the U.S. economy. Because MAP and FMD receive most of USDA's market development funding—about 90 percent in 2012—we focused our review primarily on participation in these two programs. Appendix III provides participant expenditure data on the three smaller programs—the Emerging Markets Program (EMP), the Quality Samples Program (QSP), and the Technical Assistance for Specialty Crops Program (TASC).

We analyzed USDA's market development program expenditure data for participants in each of the five programs for 2002 through 2011. We also reviewed key agency and program participant documents, including program regulations and guidelines and selected participant applications and strategies. We interviewed FAS officials in Washington, D.C., and at Agricultural Trade Offices in Japan and Mexico. We also met with several program participants in their domestic headquarters and with their overseas representatives in Japan and Mexico, where we observed some market promotion and maintenance activities. We assessed a random but nongeneralizeable sample of participants' annual progress reports, using FAS and GAO criteria for performance measures. In addition, we used FAS expenditure data to develop the sample of progress reports from 20 participants and a specific country where they were active in 2008, 2009, and 2010, for a total of 60 country progress reports. On the basis of electronic and manual data testing and interviews with knowledgeable USDA staff members, we determined that the data were sufficiently reliable for our purposes. Further, we analyzed FAS's cost-benefit analyses of MAP and FMD evaluating the impact of these programs on the U.S. economy, and we interviewed agency officials, consultants, and academics involved in these analyses. Finally, we reviewed relevant research about the economic impacts of FAS's market development programs, reviewed Office of Management and Budget guidance for

---

[3]Global Insight, Inc., *A Cost-Benefit Analysis of USDA's International Market Development Programs,* 2007. FAS also commissioned Global Insight, Inc., to perform an updated analysis, which was completed in 2010.

conducting cost-benefit analyses, and reviewed GAO's cost estimation guide. (For a full description of our scope and methodology, see app. I.)

We conducted this performance audit from August 2012 to July 2013 in accordance with generally accepted government auditing standards. Those standards require that we plan and perform the audit to obtain sufficient, appropriate evidence to provide a reasonable basis for our findings and conclusions based on our audit objectives. We believe that the evidence obtained provides a reasonable basis for our findings and conclusions based on our audit objectives.

Background

FAS administers USDA's five market development programs on behalf of the Commodity Credit Corporation, which is owned and operated by the U.S. government. The programs provide matching funds to support U.S. industry efforts to build, maintain, and expand commercial overseas markets for U.S. agricultural products, with the overarching goal of increasing agricultural exports.[4] Congress authorizes a maximum level of the corporation's funds to be used for USDA's market development programs, with the exception of QSP, through 5-year farm bills.[5] (Table 1 shows authorizations for the five programs for fiscal years 2002 through 2012.) Many other countries also provide government funding to promote

---

[4]The market development programs are funded through the permanent borrowing authority of the Commodity Credit Corporation, which was created in 1933. The corporation has permanent authority to borrow up to $30 billion at any one time from the U.S. Treasury, which it uses to finance USDA's export programs as well as its domestic price- and income-support programs.

[5]For example, title III of the Food, Conservation, and Energy Act of 2008 set the maximum funding levels for all but the QSP program through 2012 (Pub. L. No. 110-246, Title III, subtitle B, 122 Stat. 1651, 1831-34). Congress subsequently maintained these levels through a continuing resolution for 2013, pending passage of a new farm bill. See Continuing Appropriations Resolution, 2013, Pub. L. No. 112-175, 126 Stat. 1313; and Consolidated and Further Continuing Appropriations Act, 2013, Pub. L. No. 113-6, § 714, 127 Stat. 198, 227. The maximum level of annual Commodity Credit Corporation funds for QSP—$2.5 million—was set in a *Federal Register* notice in 1999 (64 Fed. Reg. 61814 [Nov. 15, 1999]).

agricultural exports that compete with U.S exports in the world market.[6] The World Trade Organization does not consider such expenditures to be trade distorting and therefore does not restrict these expenditures, according to USDA officials.

Table 1: Authorizations for USDA Market Development Programs, Fiscal Years 2002-2012

Dollars in Millions

Program	2002	2003	2004	2005	2006	2007	2008	2009	2010	2011	2012
MAP	$100	$110	$125	$140	$200	$200	$200	$200	$200	$200	$200
FMD	34.5	34.5	34.5	34.5	34.5	34.5	34.5	34.5	34.5	34.5	34.5
EMP	NA	10	10	10	10	10	10	10	10	10	10
TASC	2	2	2	2	2	2	4	7	8	9	9
QSP	2	2	2	2	2	2	2	2	2	2	2
Total	$138.5	$158.5	$173.5	$188.5	$248.5	$248.5	$250.5	$253.5	$254.5	$255.5	$255.5

Source: USDA.

MAP = Market Access Program

FMD = Foreign Market Development Program

EMP = Emerging Markets Program

TASC = Technical Assistance for Specialty Crops Program

QSP = Quality Samples Program

Participants in these programs include nonprofit agricultural trade associations; agricultural cooperatives that promote their own brand name; and state regional trade groups.[7] The majority of market

---

[6]A group of organizations, led by the U.S. Wheat Associates and representing a range of agricultural commodities, commissioned a study, which was completed in May 2013, of 12 key competitor countries' export development programs. The study found that these 12 countries, which included 4 European Union (EU) countries, spent an estimated U.S. $700 million in public funds and $1.1 billion in industry funds for a total of $1.8 billion in 2011. See Agralytica, *An Analysis of Competitor Countries' Market Development Programs: A Summary Report Prepared for Cooperator Organizations Led by U.S. Wheat Associates* (Alexandria, Va.: May 2013).

[7]These agricultural cooperatives represent large numbers of individual producers ranging from 300 for Sunsweet Growers to 6,000 for Sunkist Growers. State regional trade groups are nonprofit associations of state-funded agricultural promotion agencies, typically a state's own department of agriculture. They cover different geographic regions of the United States and allocate MAP funds to small businesses seeking to promote brand name products for export. The four state regional trade groups are the Food Export Association of the Midwest USA, Food Export USA–Northeast, Southern United States Trade Association, and the Western U.S. Agricultural Trade Association.

development funds are used for promotion of generic U.S. commodities, with no emphasis on a particular brand; however a portion of MAP funds may be used for promotion of branded products. When considering applications for funding, FAS gives priority to applicants with the broadest producer representation and affiliated industry participation of the commodity being promoted. Appendix II shows participants in the five market development programs in fiscal year 2012 and their award amounts. These organizations may participate in more than one of the five market development programs.

After approving an application for participation in a market development program, FAS sets the participant's funding level and signs a program agreement with the participant. FAS provides a program approval letter, which outlines approved activities and their budget levels, and program funds are expended through reimbursement of the participant's expense claims for approved activities. The five programs have different requirements related to participants' matching contributions, which FAS refers to as "cost-sharing"; these requirements ensure that program funds are supplemental. MAP requires participants that receive funding for promotion of generic products to make contributions to the program that are worth at least 10 percent of the funding they receive, although FAS encourages participants to commit in their program applications to contributing more than the minimum required. Eligible contributions include cash; the cost of acquiring materials; and in-kind contributions, such as professional staff time spent on design and execution of activities. The MAP branded products program and FMD require participants to make a minimum contribution of 50 percent. EMP, TASC, and QSP do not require minimum or maximum contributions, but applicants are expected to propose the amount they will contribute. For all five programs, the contribution levels that participants commit to is an important factor FAS considers in approving applications for funding, according to FAS officials. In addition, MAP and FMD participants must certify that program funds supplement, and do not supplant, any private funds, while applications for the other three programs must state why the applicants could not achieve their objectives without government funds.

In addition to having different contribution requirements, the five market development programs have different funding levels, objectives, and criteria for approving applications for funding.

- **Market Access Program.** MAP is the largest of the five programs, with a current annual authorization of $200 million—about 80 percent of USDA's total annual market development funding. In fiscal year

2012, 66 program participants received MAP awards, which ranged from about $17,000 to almost $20 million (see app. II). MAP was established in 1985 to aid in the development, expansion, and maintenance of foreign markets for U.S. agricultural commodities and products by sharing the costs of overseas marketing and promotional activities.[8] A portion of MAP funds is used for promotion of brand-name products by cooperatives or by small, for-profit businesses that apply through state regional trade groups or other MAP participants.[9] In addition, unlike participants in the MAP generic products program, small businesses promoting branded products are subject to a "graduation requirement," which limits them to no more than 5 years of promotions in a given country.[10] The MAP regulations for market development for generic and branded products identify eligible expenditures and criteria that FAS is to consider in approving applications and determining funding levels.[11] Eligible expenditures include, among others, advertising, point-of-sale materials, in-store and food service promotions and product demonstrations, seminars and educational training, participation in trade shows, market

---

[8]MAP was initially established as the Targeted Export Assistance (TEA) program in the Food Security Act of 1985. See Pub. L. No. 99-198, § 1124, 99 Stat. 1354. TEA was replaced with the Market Promotion Program (MPP) by the Food, Agriculture, Conservation, and Trade (FACT) Act of 1990. See Pub. L. No. 101-624, §§ 1531, 1572(3), 104 Stat. 3674 (amending the Agricultural Trade Act of 1978, Pub. L. No. 95-501, 92 Stat. 1685). MPP was then renamed the Market Access Program (MAP) by the Federal Agriculture Improvement and Reform (FAIR) Act of 1996. See Pub. L. No. 104-127, § 244, 110 Stat. 888.

[9]See 7 C.F.R. § 1485.15. Where the Commodity Credit Corporation approves a MAP Participant's application to run a brand promotion program that will include brand participants, the MAP Participant shall enter into participation agreements with brand participants. These agreements must include a written certification by the brand participant that it is either a small-sized entity as defined by the U.S. Small Business regulations (13 C.F.R. part 121) or a U.S. agricultural cooperative.

[10]The 5 years need not be consecutive. FAS does not consider participation in certain international trade shows in foreign countries when it is determining whether participants in the branded products program have spent 5 years in a given country. In addition, FAS exempts cooperatives from the requirement. FAS determined in 1998 that continued support for U.S. agricultural cooperatives was necessary to meet MAP's objectives, and that determination remains in place.

[11]See 7 C.F.R. §§ 1485.14 and 1485.17. Prior to May 17, 2012, the MAP regulation regarding eligible expenditures was published at 7 C.F.R. § 1485.16. The MAP regulations also require MAP participants that operate a branded product program to establish operational procedures that include their own criteria for reviewing branded companies' applications for MAP funds (see 7 C.F.R. § 1485.15).

research, and independent evaluations and audits. The process for approving applications for MAP funding involves applying a variety of qualitative criteria, including the adequacy of the applicant's plan for addressing market constraints and opportunities, prior export promotion experience, past program results, and the suitability of the applicant's plan for performance measurement. The MAP regulations also list quantitative criteria for determining award amounts for qualified applicants, including the size of the budget request relative to the projected value of exports of the commodity being promoted, the size of the budget request relative to the actual value of exports of the commodity in prior years, and the applicant's proposed contribution level.[12]

- **Foreign Market Development Program.** FMD, which was established in 1954, provides $34.5 million per year to nonprofit agricultural associations representing U.S. agricultural producers and processors, to create, expand, and maintain long-term export markets primarily for generic bulk commodities. In fiscal year 2012, 24 FMD participants received award amounts ranging from about $16,000 to more than $5 million (see app. II).[13] FMD allows many of the same expenditures as MAP, such as market research and product demonstrations; however, unlike MAP, FMD funds may not be used for activities targeted directly at consumers. The qualitative criteria for approving applications for participation in FMD and the quantitative factors for determining award amounts are also similar to those for MAP. Examples of these quantitative factors include the applicant's contribution level and the value of exports being promoted.[14]

---

[12]7 C.F.R. § 1485.14(c).

[13]FMD was first established by the Agricultural Trade Development and Assistance Act of 1954 and was reauthorized in 1996 by an amendment to Title VII of the Agricultural Trade Act of 1978. See Pub.L. No. 480, ch. 469, 68 Stat. 454; and Federal Agriculture Improvement and Reform Act of 1996, Pub. L. No. 104-127, Title II, § 252, 110 Stat. 888, 972.

[14]The FMD regulations and the *Federal Register Notice of Funds Availability for FMD* list the specific criteria that FAS is to use in approving applications for funding and setting award amounts. See 7 C.F.R. §§ 1484.21 - 22 and 78 Fed. Reg. 23,889-23,890 (Apr. 23, 2013).

- **Emerging Markets Program.** EMP, which was established in 1990, provides up to $10 million annually[15] to U.S private-sector, university, or government entities for technical assistance activities intended to promote exports of U.S. agricultural commodities and products in emerging markets by improving their food and business systems and reducing potential trade barriers.[16] In 2012, FAS awarded EMP funds to 35 entities, some of which received funding for more than one EMP project, with total awards per participant ranging from $14,000 to about $500,000 (see app. II). Types of projects funded may include feasibility studies, market research, sector assessments, orientation visits, specialized training, business workshops, and similar undertakings. EMP is not intended for projects targeted at end-user consumers. Ineligible expenses include branded product promotions (e.g., in-store promotions, restaurant advertising, labeling); advertising, administrative, and operational expenses for trade shows; website development; equipment purchases; and the preparation and printing of brochures, flyers, and posters. The EMP regulations list the criteria FAS is to consider in reviewing applications for funding.[17] Among these criteria are the applicant's willingness to contribute resources; the degree to which the proposed project is likely to contribute to the development, maintenance, or expansion of U.S. agricultural exports to emerging markets; and a demonstration of how the proposed project will benefit a particular industry as a whole. Individual projects are unlikely to be approved at levels above $500,000, and funding for continuing and substantially similar projects is generally limited to 3 years.

- **Quality Samples Program.** QSP, which was established in 1999, currently provides $2 million annually to assist U.S. organizations in

---

[15]EMP's initial authorization of $5 million is found in section 1542 of the Food, Agriculture, Conservation, and Trade Act of 1990 (Pub. L. No. 101-624, § 1542).

[16]EMP regulation defines an emerging market as any country or regional grouping that is taking steps toward a market-oriented economy through the food, agriculture, or rural business sectors of the economy of the country; has the potential to provide a viable and significant market for U.S. agricultural commodities or products; and has a population greater than $1 million and a per capita income level below the level for upper-middle-income countries as determined by the World Bank (7 C.F.R. § 1486.101). The World Bank periodically redefines the income limits on upper-middle-income economies. Consequently, an absolute list of emerging markets has not been established.

[17]7 C.F.R. § 1486.209.

supplying commodity samples to potential foreign importers.[18] Projects focus on industry and manufacturing, rather than on end-use consumers, and are intended to promote U.S. food and fiber products. In fiscal year 2012, 12 program participants received QSP funding, in most cases for multiple projects, with total awards per participant ranging from $5,000 to $460,000 (see app. II). QSP funding for individual projects is limited to $75,000, and the projects should be completed within a year of approval by FAS. Eligible expenditures include the sample purchase price and the cost of transporting the samples domestically to the port of export and from there to the foreign port or point-of-entry. Samples provided in a QSP project may not be directly used as part of a retail promotion or supplied directly to consumers. The annual QSP Notice of Funds Availability spells out the criteria that FAS is to use for approving applications for QSP funding.[19] These criteria include, among others, the potential for expanding commercial sales in the proposed market; the importer's contribution in terms of handling and processing the sample; the amount of funding requested and the applicant's willingness to contribute resources; and how well the proposal's technical assistance will demonstrate the intended end-use benefit.

- **Technical Assistance for Specialty Crops Program.**[20] TASC, which was established in 2002, is currently authorized under the 2008 farm bill, as extended by the American Tax Payer Relief Act of 2012, to provide a maximum of $9 million to U.S. entities, for projects that address sanitary, phytosanitary, and technical barriers that prohibit or

---

[18]QSP is authorized under Section 5(f) of the Commodity Credit Corporation Charter Act, codified as amended at 15 U.S.C. § 714c (f).

[19]See *Notice of Funds Availability: Inviting Applications for the Quality Samples Program*, 78 Fed. Reg. 23,896 (Apr. 23, 2013).

[20]TASC regulations (7 C.F.R. § 1487.1) define specialty crops as all cultivated plants, or the products thereof, produced in the United States, except wheat, feed grains, oilseeds, cotton, rice, peanuts, sugar, and tobacco.

limit U.S. specialty crop exports.[21] Any U.S. organization may receive TASC funding, including, but not limited to, U.S. government and state government agencies, nonprofit trade associations, universities, agricultural cooperatives, and private businesses. In 2012, FAS awarded funds to 24 participants, some of whom received funding for multiple projects, and total funding awarded to each participant ranged from about $1.3 million to $14,000 (see app. II). FAS will not consider proposals for TASC funding that exceed $500,000 in a given year. Examples of eligible expenditures include seminars and workshops, study tours, field surveys, development of pest lists, and pest and disease research. Certain types of expenses are not eligible for reimbursement, such as the costs of market research, advertising, and other promotional expenses. The TASC regulations list a variety of criteria that FAS is to consider in evaluating applications for funding, including, among others, the viability and completeness of the proposal, the potential trade impact of the project on issues such as market retention, and the cost and level of contributions from the applicant.[22]

Participants in MAP and FMD Have Remained Relatively Consistent in Recent Years

Participants in USDA's market development programs use program funds to support a variety of activities intended to raise awareness or acceptance of U.S. agricultural products in overseas markets. MAP and FMD participants, their share of program expenditures, and the countries where they spent the majority of program funds remained relatively consistent from 2007 through 2011. Unlike funds for the other programs, a portion of MAP funds is used for promotion of branded products. In 2011, MAP participants spent about 85 percent of program funding on overseas promotion of generic commodities; more than 600 small companies and seven agricultural cooperatives spent the remaining 15 percent of MAP funding to promote branded products. MAP and FMD participants met or exceeded those programs' requirements for minimum

---

[21]TASC was first established in the Farm Security and Rural Investment Act of 2002 (Pub. L. No. 107–171, § 3205, 116 Stat. 134, 301). Section 701 of the American Taxpayer Relief Act of 2012 extended certain authorities and amendments made by the 2008 farm bill including the authority for TASC. See Pub. L. No. 112-240, § 701, 126 Stat. 2313, 2362 (2013). Sanitary and phytosanitary measures are rules and procedures that governments adopt to ensure that imported foods and beverages are safe to consume and to protect domestic animals and plants from pests and diseases. Technical barriers to trade are nontariff trade barriers that can take the form of product standards, testing requirements, and other technical requirements.

[22]7 C.F.R. § 1487.6(a).

GAO-13-740 Agricultural Trade

matching contributions. Appendix III shows EMP, QSP, and TASC participant expenditures in 2011.

Program Participants Have Conducted a Variety of Activities to Promote Their Products Overseas

Market development program participants have used program funds to conduct a variety of activities intended to raise awareness or acceptance of U.S. agricultural products in overseas markets. Participants have also used program funds to address technical barriers that prohibit or limit specialty crop exports. Many program participants receive funding from more than one of the five market development programs. For instance, in fiscal year 2012, 22 of the 66 MAP participants received funds from FMD, and 22 of the 24 FMD participants received funds from MAP. In addition, all 12 QSP participants, 6 of the 24 TASC participants, and 18 of the 35 EMP participants received funds from at least one other program (see app. II for additional details). The following paragraphs present examples of five participants' use of 2011 program funds for market development efforts in Japan and Mexico.[23] Common activities undertaken included, among others, market research, consumer and retail promotion, participation in international trade shows, and reverse trade missions, in which foreign buyers visit U.S. agricultural producers.

[23]The five participants we selected for our case studies received MAP, FMD, or TASC funds in 2011, in some cases receiving funds from more than one program; none of the five participants received EMP or QSP funds in that year. See appendix I for a description of our selection of the five participants for the case studies.

Figure 1: Examples of Market Development Activities

In-store advertisement for California table grapes.

Source: California Table Grape Commission.

Importers and distributors at a Wine Institute promotion event in Mexico City.

Source: GAO.

Japanese retailers visiting U.S. cotton field.

Source: Cotton Council International.

American Hardwood Export Council

The American Hardwood Export Council used more than $1.7 million in 2011 MAP and FMD funds for multiple generic product promotional efforts in Japan. According to a council representative, consumers in Japan value wood products from trees that are harvested legally and sustainably, which provides a marketing advantage for American hardwood compared with woods from tropical competitors. We visited furniture stores in Japan displaying the American Hardwood Export Council's informational handouts, which highlight the sustainability and legality of American hardwoods used in the furniture. The council's efforts in Japan also include educating designers and architects about the environmental advantage—that is, the smaller carbon "footprint"—of sustainable wood products compared with synthetic material. The council also conducts educational efforts aimed at explaining to Japanese furniture and flooring manufacturers, designers, and architects that discoloration and curving grains are wood characteristics rather than imperfections, because, according to a council representative, straight wood grain has traditionally been favored in Japan.

California Table Grape Commission

California Table Grape Commission used about $271,000 in 2011 MAP funds for generic product promotional activities in Mexico. Commission representatives informed us that in-store promotional activities are the most effective means of reaching the customer. Promotional activities include in-store grape display competitions as well as promotions with other U.S. fruit groups, such as apples and pears. The commission also used MAP funding to conduct in-store grape sampling demonstrations at major retail chains throughout Mexico to demonstrate the quality of California grapes. In 2010 and 2011, FAS authorized the commission to use TASC funds for activities to remove, resolve, or mitigate sanitary, phytosanitary, and related barriers that prohibit or threaten the export of U.S. specialty crops in multiple countries. In 2011, the commission received an allocation of more than $363,000 for a multiyear TASC project to conduct research and provide the ancillary staffing and supplies needed to identify postharvest treatment protocols to eliminate invasive pests in U.S. grape exports.

Cotton Council International

Cotton Council International used more than $2.7 million in MAP and FMD funds in 2011 for generic product promotion activities in Japan. These activities—such as educating Japanese consumers about the benefits and unique characteristics of cotton versus other fibers and conducting advertising, public relations, and promotions—were intended to increase consumer preference for cotton and retailer demand for fabrics made from U.S. cotton. According to representatives from Cotton Council International, increasing demand for clothing made with U.S. cotton in a large consumer market, such as Japan, also increases exports of cotton fiber to other countries that manufacture cotton garments for sale to retail buyers in Japan.

Western United States Agricultural Trade Association

The Western United States Agricultural Trade Association (WUSATA) provided a total of about $926,000 in MAP funds for market development activities in Japan and Mexico in 2011. WUSATA, which is one of four state regional trade groups with responsibility for supporting MAP branded product promotion for small businesses, directed more than half of this funding to 34 small businesses to support their branded product promotions in Japan and Mexico. WUSATA allocates the majority of its annual MAP funds to more than 200 small businesses and cooperatives based in 13 western states, according to WUSATA officials. WUSATA also uses some of its MAP funds for generic product promotion, primarily for participation in numerous international trade shows and for inbound and outbound trade missions. In addition, WUSATA devotes some MAP funding for generic product promotion and outreach efforts to small businesses to encourage them to consider exporting their products and use assistance from the MAP program. WUSATA officials noted that many businesses are unaware of their products' overseas market potential.

Wine Institute

The Wine Institute used more than $106,000 in 2011 MAP funds for generic product promotional activities in Mexico. In Mexico, we observed a Wine Institute-sponsored promotional event in Mexico City to facilitate trade contacts between California wine label representatives and Mexican wine importers. The event was intended to generate publicity for California wines and increase consumer awareness. In Japan, where consumers are most familiar with European wines, the Wine Institute worked with restaurants to promote California wines, according to a Wine Institute representative. The Wine Institute uses some of its MAP funding to support branded product promotion by small businesses. In 2011, the Wine Institute also received a $500,000 TASC allocation for a 5-year project to prepare and file petitions to the Japanese government to allow the sale of U.S. wines containing certain additives that are commonly used by U.S. producers.

MAP and FMD Program Participants and Expenditures Remained Generally Consistent in Program Years 2007 through 2011

MAP and FMD participants and their share of market development program expenditures remained relatively consistent from 2007 through 2011, with many of the same participants receiving the majority of funding each year. Expenditures by the 10 participants that spent the largest amounts of funding from the two programs in 2011 represented 54 to 57 percent of those programs' total expenditures in 2007 through 2011 (see table 2).[24] According to FAS officials, these 10 participants also reflect the top 10 U.S. exports of agricultural products in 2011, although not in the

---

[24]See tables 8, 9, and 10 in appendix III for program participants with largest shares of EMP, QSP, and TASC expenditures in 2011.

same rank order. An FAS official noted that MAP and FMD typically provide ongoing support for program participants that seek not only to open new overseas markets but also to maintain export market share. These participants typically receive funding every year. According to FAS officials, although a variety of both qualitative and quantitative factors affect the level of funding provided to participants each year, FAS seeks to provide a stable level of funding to support participants' multiyear market development strategies.[25]

Table 2: Market Access Program (MAP) and Foreign Market Development Program (FMD) Expenditures in 2007-2011 for Program Participants with Largest Shares of Total 2011 Expenditures

Dollars in millions

Participant ranking by 2011 MAP and FMD expenditures	MAP participant	FMD participant	MAP and FMD expenditures				
			2007	2008	2009	2010	2011
1 Cotton Council International	yes	yes	$32	$25	$25	$25	**$24**
2 U.S. Meat Export Federation	yes	yes	17	20	18	18	**19**
3 U.S. Grains Council	yes	yes	13	12	13	14	**15**
4 AHEC, APA, SEC, SFPA[a]	yes	yes	13	13	13	13	**14**
5 U.S. Wheat Associates	yes	yes	11	11	12	12	**13**
6 Food Export Association Midwest USA	yes	no	10	11	11	11	**12**
7 American Soybean Association	yes	yes	16	14	12	10	**11**
8 Western United States Agricultural Trade Assoc.	yes	no	9	11	11	11	**10**
9 Food Export USA–Northeast	yes	no	7	8	9	9	**9**
10 Southern United States Trade Association	yes	no	7	7	6	6	**7**
Top 10 2011 MAP and FMD participants' total expenditures (percentage of all MAP and FMD expenditures)			**$134.3 (54%)**	**$130.5 (55%)**	**$129.4 (55%)**	**$129.5 (56%)**	**$134.0 (57%)**
All MAP and FMD expenditures			**$249.0**	**$238.7**	**$233.2**	**$233.0**	**$235.0**

Source: GAO analysis of USDA data.

Notes:

The participants shown represent those with the 10 highest total MAP and FMD expenditures for 2011. The same participants were among the top 15 each year in 2007 through 2010, although not always in the same rank order as in 2011.

[25]Quantitative criteria for setting funding levels include the dollar value of exports, participant contribution levels, and prior year funding levels. FAS may reduce or increase a participant's award amount depending on the quality of the participant's program or a change in conditions affecting its ability to maintain or expand exports. EMP, QSP, and TASC provide project-specific funding rather than ongoing assistance to participants.

Numbers in columns may not sum to totals because of rounding.

^aThe American Hardwood Export Council (AHEC), the Engineered Wood Association (APA), the Softwood Export Council (SEC), and the Southern Forest Products Association (SFPA) collectively submit single annual applications for MAP and FMD awards.

Majority of MAP and FMD Funding Is Spent in a Consistent Group of Countries

Our analysis of expenditure data from 2002 through 2011 shows that MAP and FMD participants spent market development funds throughout the world, consistently spending more than half of the funds in the same 10 countries. (Table 3 shows MAP and FMD expenditures in these countries in 2011.)[26] The expenditures in these 10 countries accounted for 66 percent, on average, of total MAP and FMD expenditures from 2002 through 2011. According to an FAS official, participants are encouraged to direct program funds to markets where they will have the greatest impact on increasing exports. This official noted that, although participants use MAP and FMD funds in a variety of export markets, the majority of their funds are expended in countries with the largest export markets for U.S. agricultural products.

---

[26]See table 11 in appendix III for countries where the largest amounts of EMP, QSP, and TASC funding were spent in 2011.

GAO-13-740 Agricultural Trade

Table 3: Countries Where Largest Amounts of Market Access Program (MAP) and Foreign Market Development Program (FMD) Funds Were Spent in 2011

Dollars in millions

Country ranking by share of MAP and FMD expenditures		Total MAP and FMD expenditures	Percentage of total MAP and FMD expenditures
1	Japan	$30	13%
2	China	26	11
3	Mexico	23	10
4	United Kingdom	15	6
5	United States	13	6
6	South Korea	12	5
7	Canada	10	4
8	Germany	10	4
9	Taiwan	7	3
10	Hong Kong	6	3
Total		**$153**	**65%**

Source: GAO analysis of USDA expenditure data.

Notes:

Our analysis of data for 2002 through 2011 shows that MAP and FMD participants consistently spent more than half of program funds in the 10 countries shown. The United States is included among these countries because participants spend program funding in the United States on a variety of activities, such as reverse trade missions, international trade shows, and research for select Emerging Markets Program and Technical Assistance for Specialty Crops Program projects. In addition, the strategic regional trade groups use program funds to pay for domestic administrative expenses.

Although the United States does not have diplomatic relations with Taiwan, we have listed it as a separate country because whenever the laws of the United States refer or relate to foreign countries, nations, states, governments, or similar entities, such terms shall include and shall apply to Taiwan.

Hong Kong is a special administrative region of China, but we have included it in this report as a separate country because it is an economic entity separate from the rest of China and is able to enter into international agreements on its own behalf in commercial and economic matters.

Expenditure amounts are rounded to the nearest million and therefore may not sum to column totals.

Fifteen Percent of 2011 MAP Expenditures Supported Promotion of Branded Products

In 2011, about 15 percent of total MAP expenditures were used to promote branded products. The four state regional trade groups and five of the agricultural trade associations in the MAP program allocated a portion of their MAP funding to small businesses to promote branded products in foreign markets. Specifically, these groups allocated a total of more than $22.8 million in MAP funds for branded product promotions in 2011 to 644 small businesses. These small businesses' average expenditure in 2011 was about $25,000 and their median expenditure was $33,000. Small businesses use MAP funding for a variety of activities, including participation in trade shows, buying missions, advertising, and in-store demonstrations and promotions. In addition, seven agricultural cooperatives—Sunkist Growers, Inc.; Blue Diamond Growers; Sunsweet Growers, Inc.; Sun-Maid Growers of California; Welch Foods, Inc.; Ocean Spray Cranberries, Inc.; and Cal-Pure Pistachios, Inc.—spent about $6.4 million in 2011 to promote their own brands. According to FAS officials, cooperatives' activities to promote their products using a brand name are often similar to the activities of trade associations promoting generic commodities. Table 4 shows the 16 organizations that participated in the MAP branded products program in 2011, the portions of their total MAP expenditures that were used for promotions of branded products, and the numbers of small businesses that the participants' MAP branded products program expenditures supported.

Table 4: Expenditures and Numbers of Small Businesses Supported in 2011 by Participants in Market Access Program (MAP) Branded Products Program

Dollars in thousands

Participant	Branded products program expenditures	Total MAP expenditures	Branded products program expenditures as percentage of total MAP expenditures	Number of small businesses supported through the branded program
State regional trade groups				
Food Export Association of the Midwest	$7,151	$11,561	62%	167
Western U.S. Agricultural Trade Association	7,162	10,204	70	217
Food Export USA - Northeast	4,843	9,097	53	143
Southern U.S. Trade Association	2,630	7,180	37	65
Trade associations				
U.S. Meat Export Federation	60	17,481	0.3	10
Wine Institute	89	6,372	1	6
National Confectioners Association	661	1,583	42	19
U.S. Livestock Genetics Export, Inc.	233	1,160	20	16
New York Wine and Grape Foundation	2	398	0.4	1
Cooperatives				
Almond Board of California/Blue Diamond Growers	1,326	3,755	35	NA
California Prune Board/Sunsweet Growers Inc.	698	3,196	22	NA
Sunkist Growers, Inc	2,551	2,551	100	NA
Raisin Administrative Committee/Sun Maid Growers of California	89	1,975	5	NA
Cranberry Marketing Committee/Ocean Spray Cranberries, Inc.	350	1,758	20	NA
American Pistachio Growers/Cal-Pure Pistachios Inc.	503	967	52	NA
Welch Foods Inc.	922	922	100	NA
Total	**$29,267**	**$201,242**	**15%**	**644**

Source: GAO analysis of USDA data.

Notes:

With the exception of Sunkist Growers and Welch Foods, Inc., the cooperatives shown participate in the MAP program with a partner trade association that promotes a generic commodity. For example, the Almond Board of California promotes almonds generically with its share of MAP funding, while Blue Diamond Growers uses its share of MAP funding to promote almonds with the Blue Diamond brand name.

Numbers in columns may not sum to totals because of rounding.

From 2002 through 2011, a total of 2,131 unique small businesses received funding for promotional activities through the MAP branded products program. Many of the small businesses participated in the MAP branded products program for multiple years. Of the 2,131 businesses, 41 percent were involved in the branded products program for 1 year, and 59 percent were involved for more than a year. In 2011, 153 small businesses expended MAP branded program funds for the first time. The MAP branded products program had, on average, about 638 unique small businesses per year and supported activities throughout the world. The largest expenditures of program funding for MAP branded products were directed to 8 of the 10 countries with the largest expenditures of total MAP and FMD funding, shown in table 3.

From 2002 through 2011, small businesses in the MAP branded products program reached the 5-year limit for promoting a product in a given country—known as the program's "graduation requirement"—in 1,121 instances.[27] These instances involved 569 businesses in about 80 countries. During this period, 64 businesses used MAP branded products program funding for more than 5 years in a given country in 82 instances. According to FAS, participation in certain international trade shows is exempt from the graduation requirement for the MAP branded products program.[28]

---

[27]The graduation requirement applies only to small businesses eligible to participate in the MAP branded products program. FAS waives the graduation requirement for participating agricultural cooperatives.

[28]Current MAP regulations state that small businesses participating in certain international trade shows in foreign countries will not be considered when determining their time in country for purposes of the 5-year graduation requirement. Such shows must meet two criteria: (1) They are food or agricultural shows, with no less than 30 percent of exhibitors selling food or agricultural products, and are international shows—that is, targeting buyers, distributors, and the like from more than one foreign country. (2) No fewer than 15 percent of each show's visitors are from countries other than the host country (7 C.F.R. § 1485,15). FAS regularly compiles a list of international trade shows that are exempt from the graduation requirement and publishes the list as a MAP notice on FAS's website.

Matching Contributions for MAP and FMD Met or Exceeded Minimum Contribution Requirements in 2011

In 2011, all MAP and FMD participants met or exceeded the programs' required minimum matching contribution levels.[29] The average contribution level for MAP participants was about 191 percent of MAP expenditures in 2011, and the median contribution level was about 134 percent.[30] The majority of these participants contributed more than 100 percent of their total expenditures. The average contribution level for all FMD participants in 2011 was 316 percent, and the median was 232 percent. Nearly all FMD participants provided matching cash and in-kind contributions of more than 100 percent of total expenditures.

Since 2002, MAP participants' total contributions have ranged from 138 percent to 198 percent of their total MAP expenditures, and FMD participants' total contributions have ranged from 123 percent to 192 percent of their total FMD expenditures. Table 5 compares MAP and FMD participants' contributions and expenditures in 2002 through 2011.

---

[29]The minimum contribution requirement for a participant in the MAP generic products program is 10 percent of the participant's MAP expenditures; the requirement for a participant in the MAP branded product program is 50 percent of total expenditures. FMD also requires a minimum contribution of 50 percent of resources provided by FAS; all FMD promotion is for generic commodities. Small businesses in the MAP branded products program are reimbursed for 50 percent of their expenses for approved activities.

[30]The average MAP participant contribution and expenditure levels reflect contributions and expenditures for both generic and branded product promotions.

Table 5: Market Access Program (MAP) and Foreign Market Development Program (FMD) Participants' Total Contributions and Expenditures, 2002–2011

Dollars in millions

	Participant contributions	Participant expenditures	Contributions as percentage of expenditures
MAP			
2002	$199	$101	198%
2003	193	129	150
2004	207	140	148
2005	347	234	148
2007	318	213	149
2008	349	204	171
2009	274	199	138
2010	330	201	164
2011	394	201	196
FMD			
2002	$45	$31	146%
2003	46	33	140
2004	44	36	123
2005	51	37	139
2006	49	35	137
2007	49	36	137
2008	52	35	150
2009	60	34	176
2010	62	32	192
2011	62	34	184

Source: GAO analysis of USDA data.

Notes:

In 2006, FAS changed the MAP program year timeframe. As a result, FAS recorded 2006 MAP expenditures and contributions among data for the 2005 and 2007 program years, according to an FAS official.

Participants in the MAP generic and branded products programs are required to contribute a minimum of 10 percent and 50 percent, respectively, of their program expenditures. Participants in FMD are required to contr bute a minimum of 50 percent of resources received from FAS.

FAS Uses Management Processes to Reduce Duplication Risks, but Some Participants' Annual Progress Reports Have Not Identified Assessment Methodologies

FAS has established processes to reduce risks of duplication among the five market development programs, to monitor participant expenditures, and to assess program results. FAS's integrated approach includes a unified database and application process to help mitigate risks of duplication. In addition, FAS works with participants in the MAP branded products program to ensure that the small businesses they support are not receiving funds for similar activities from more than one source; our review of 2011 data found no small businesses receiving funds from multiple sources. FAS also conducts regular compliance reviews to verify participants' program expenditures and contributions. FAS guidelines require program participants to submit annual progress reports assessing results for each country where they conduct market development activities. In the progress reports that we reviewed, program participants' performance measures generally reflected requirements in FAS guidelines as well as key attributes of successful performance measurement that we identified in previous GAO reports. However, 149 of the 373 performance measures in the reports that we reviewed did not clearly identify, as the FAS guidelines require, the methodologies used to assess results for each performance measure, making it difficult to verify the reported results. FAS guidelines also require MAP and FMD participants to conduct comprehensive evaluations of their program-funded market development activities when appropriate.

FAS Established Integrated Management Processes to Reduce Risks of Duplication among Market Development Programs

FAS integrates its management processes to reduce the risk of duplication among the market development programs, given that many participants receive funding from more than one program. Because MAP and FMD support many of the same goals and allowable expenses and most FMD participants also participate in MAP, the greatest risk of duplication is between these two programs. To reduce this risk, FAS uses an integrated online system, known as the Unified Export Strategy (UES) system, which participants typically use to apply for funding for any of the five market development programs.[31] For example, a participant seeking funding for both FMD and MAP submits a single application through the

---

[31]UES is a standardized online Internet system developed by USDA and available for use by entities to apply to any USDA market development program. FAS encourages participants to submit their applications through the UES system, but does not require them to do so. According to an FAS official, participants generally apply through the UES system. In some cases applicants for relatively small projects may submit applications outside the UES system; however, FAS tracks all approved activities and expenditures through the system.

UES system, explaining how it intends to use both programs to support its foreign market development objectives. FAS's review of these funding applications allows it to prevent duplicative programming, according to FAS officials. FAS officials also noted that only expenses for pre-approved activities may be reimbursed and that the UES system associates each approved activity with the particular program for which it was approved. In addition, FAS agricultural attachés based in overseas posts review and comment on the portions of participants' applications that apply to their countries and regions. This provides an additional layer of review that helps prevent duplicative programming, according to FAS officials.

FAS also takes steps to ensure that small businesses participating in the MAP branded program do not obtain funding from more than one source—such as two state regional trade groups—for promotion in the same country. To prevent such duplicative funding, FAS requires that the four state regional trade groups provide the names of all businesses and products participating in their branded promotion programs each year.[32] According to an FAS official, FAS also participates in regular conference calls with the four state regional trade groups, during which they compare lists of small businesses applying for branded products program funding. In addition, FAS circulates a memo annually to the four groups, stating that businesses that promote certain product types should seek funding from specific commodity groups before applying for funds from the state regional trade groups. For example, FAS's memo in 2012 stated that small businesses promoting dairy, livestock, meat, poultry, seafood, and egg products should be referred first to the applicable commodity groups before applying for funding from a state regional trade group. In reviewing expenditure data for MAP branded product promotions for the 2011 program year, we found no instances in which small businesses obtained funding from multiple sources to promote the same products in the same countries.

---

[32]According to an FAS official, a small business may obtain funding for branded product promotion from more than one program participant—either a trade association or a state regional trade group—if the business uses the second source of funding in different countries or for different products.

FAS Monitors Participants' Expenses for All Programs through Its Compliance Review Process

FAS performs financial and compliance reviews to verify that participants claimed reimbursement for expenses appropriately, and it holds participants accountable for maintaining proper documentation of all of their reimbursement claims. According to an FAS official, FAS's independent Compliance Review Branch has a staff of eight officers, including the branch chief, who periodically visit participant sites to verify that all expenses submitted for reimbursement are authorized, reasonable, and documented. These compliance reviews cover all market development programs in which the participant was involved, enabling the compliance officers to verify that all reimbursement claims were paid for pre-approved expenses for each program. The reviews also verify that participants' reported contributions are properly documented, are based on allowable expenses, and match the amounts that the participants committed to in their market development program applications. In addition, the compliance officers verify that participants that spent $500,000 or more of federal funds from one or more sources in a single year have been audited in accordance with Office of Management and Budget Circular A-133. Our review of FAS documentation for five program participants showed that FAS conducted compliance reviews of these participants between May 2011 and March 2012.

According to the Compliance Review Branch Chief, compliance officers typically conduct these reviews every 3 years for the smaller participants and verify 100 percent of those participants' expenses. Compliance officers conduct reviews more frequently for the larger participants because of the volume of reimbursement claims involved, and they may review only a sample of those participants' expenses. Participants must return to FAS any reimbursements for claims found not to be allowable. The Compliance Review Branch Chief stated that, although participants have the right to a hearing to contest compliance review results, they generally repay the rejected claims under an agreed timeframe. The Chief also noted that, because participants typically apply for future funding from the programs, they have an incentive to comply with FAS requirements.

Selected MAP and FMD Progress Reports Generally Reflected FAS Requirements and Key Attributes of Successful Performance Measurement, but Some Reports Did Not Identify Assessment Methodology as Required

The performance measures in the progress reports that we reviewed generally met criteria based on FAS guidance for progress reports and key attributes of successful performance measures that we previously identified. However, some participants' annual progress reports did not identify the approaches and information sources used to assess activity results for each performance measure, as FAS guidelines require. FAS guidelines require MAP and FMD participants to submit, within 6 months after the program year ends, annual country progress reports identifying market challenges, describing activities over the past year, and stating measureable goals and results of their performance.[33] These reports enable the participants and FAS to assess the participants' progress in achieving their stated goals each year. In addition, FAS considers participants' progress reports when reviewing their MAP and FMD funding applications for subsequent years.

FAS Has Established Guidance for Developing and Reviewing Annual Progress Reports

FAS guidelines require, among other things, that MAP and FMD participants' annual progress reports contain the following elements to demonstrate how their market development activities are relevant and their impact is measured.[34] The reports should identify "constraints"—that is, obstacles to achieving stated objectives—and "opportunities," which participants can utilize to achieve their objectives in the markets where they operate. The reports should also provide the performance measures that will be used to assess each activity's impact on these constraints and opportunities. (See the text box for an example, from FAS guidelines, of a constraint and its related performance measures.) Further, the reports should show, for each performance measure, an associated baseline measure, a stated goal for the given year, and a result. Finally, the reports should identify the methodology that will be used to assess progress toward the goal associated with each performance measure.

---

[33]FAS has different reporting requirements for EMP and TASC participants than for MAP and FMD participants. We reviewed only progress reports associated with MAP and FMD programs, which represent the vast majority of FAS's market development funding.

[34]Agralytica, *Results-Oriented Management: A Guide for FAS Industry Partners* (Alexandria, Va.: 2001).

> **FAS Example of a Constraint and Associated Performance Measures for a Hypothetical Seafood Group**
>
> *Constraint: [Seafood products are] new products for [Country X], and their availability and characteristics...are not known by the three major retailers. Also, [the retailers] are not aware of their potential consumer interest in these species and how they can increase their profits by introducing them.*
>
> Performance measures associated with the constraint:
>
> - Number of retailers carrying targeted regional U.S. products on a regular basis
> - Number of new products sampled by targeted retailers
> - Number of products carried on a regular basis by targeted retailers
> - Sales to targets
>
> Source: Agralytica, *Results-Oriented Management: A Guide for FAS Industry Partners* (Alexandria, Va.: 2001).

FAS staff in Washington, D.C., and at applicable overseas posts review participants' annual progress reports as part of the annual application review, according to FAS officials and participant representatives. FAS staff provide feedback to participants about their reports both informally, through e-mail and telephone, and formally, through feedback letters. For example, one feedback letter from FAS that we reviewed instructed the participant to express its objectives more concisely and to develop performance measures that track the desired outcome rather than the participant's activities. FAS officials noted that their reviews of funding applications consider whether participants adjusted their market development strategies on the basis of results they reported for the previous year. Two Agricultural Trade Officers told us that, in addition to reviewing the reports, they have provided participants support and feedback regarding the identification of constraints and opportunities and development of performance measures.

FAS also provides training to help participants identify constraints and opportunities and develop performance measures that meet FAS's requirements. According to FAS officials, biannual conferences of program participants generally include workshops on program evaluation, which in the past have emphasized developing meaningful performance measures. One of the Agricultural Trade Officers whom we interviewed reported having conducted a workshop that reviewed the UES process and discussed key definitions and criteria for identifying constraints and opportunities and for developing performance measures.

Selected Participants' Progress Reports Generally Reflected FAS Requirements and Key Attributes of Successful Performance Measurement, but Some Did Not Identify Methods Used to Assess Results

The country progress reports that we reviewed generally complied with criteria based on selected FAS guidelines for preparing progress reports[35] and key attributes of successful performance measurement that we had previously identified.[36] In general, the 56 reports by MAP and FMD participants that we reviewed[37] met five of six criteria we used for our analysis.[38] However, 149 of the 373 performance measures in the sampled reports (40 percent) did not identify the methodologies used to assess results, as FAS guidelines require. Following are details of our analysis of the performance measures in the progress reports we reviewed, using these six criteria.

1. **Constraint or opportunity has at least one outcome measure.** For each constraint or opportunity shown in a progress report, FAS guidelines require that at least one performance measure be outcome oriented rather than output oriented. FAS describes an outcome as showing changed behavior, with an emphasis on what was achieved and how participant activities have affected attitudes and consumer habits in the targeted market. In contrast, FAS defines an output as showing what was done at the activity level (e.g., two seminars conducted, newsletter sent to 1,000 addressees).[39] The progress reports that we reviewed used both outcome and output measures to determine the impact of activities and to address the identified constraints and opportunities. At least one outcome measure was

---

[35]Agralytica, *Results-Oriented Management: A Guide for FAS Industry Partners.*

[36]GAO, *Tax Administration: IRS Needs to Further Refine Its Tax Filing Season Performance Measures*, GAO-03-143 (Washington, D.C.: Nov. 22, 2002).

[37]We assessed a nongeneralizable sample of 56 progress reports, containing 378 performance measures, which were prepared by 19 MAP and FMD participants for program years 2008 through 2010. Some of the reports also provided narrative updates on program activities in one or more of the other market development programs, as applicable.

[38]For our review, we used criteria based on the FAS guidelines that FAS marketing specialists use to assess the quality of participants' country progress reports as well as on previous GAO work that identifies key attributes of successful performance measures (see GAO-03-143). For more information on our scope and methodology, see appendix I.

[39]FAS guidelines note that an output does not indicate change in understanding or attitude and should not be used as a meaningful measure of progress at either the activity or constraint levels. According to FAS officials, results of outcome measures usually reflect multiple activities and should demonstrate progress made in the market. The officials stated that these results inform evaluative feedback on a participant's entire program and impact future strategies and activities.

associated with 105 of the 115 constraints and opportunities in the sample (91 percent), and outcome measures constituted 260 of the 378 performance measures (69 percent).[40]

2. **Performance measure is clear.** We assessed the clarity of the performance measures. Specifically, we assessed whether the measure's name and definition were clearly stated and consistent with the numerical goal used to calculate it—a key attribute for successful performance measures that we previously identified.[41] We found that 356 of the 378 performance measures (94 percent) in the progress reports that we reviewed met this criterion.

3. **Performance measure is aligned with related constraint or opportunity.** To ensure alignment of performance measures with the constraints or opportunities they address, FAS guidelines state that each measure must directly affect the related constraint or opportunity, must reflect the scope of activity and progress in the market, and must be within the ability of the participants to influence. In the progress reports that we reviewed, 330 of the 378 performance measures (87 percent) were aligned with the related constraint or opportunity, and 110 of the 118 constraints and opportunities had at least one aligned performance measure associated with it. However, 58 (13 percent) of the performance measures were not aligned with a constraint or opportunity, indicating a risk that those participants might measure incorrectly, or fail to measure, the impact of their activities.[42]

4. **Performance measure is quantifiable.** FAS guidelines require that each performance measure be quantifiable. All 378 (100 percent) of the measures in the sample of progress reports we reviewed were quantifiable, with numerical values. When a goal is measurable, FAS

---

[40]We were unable to determine whether 6 percent of the performance measures were output or outcome measures. Although FAS provides definitions for outputs and outcomes in its guidance, the contractors who developed the model and guidance acknowledged that it can be difficult to differentiate an output from an outcome.

[41]GAO-03-143.

[42]For example, if a participant's constraint was a lack of awareness of a certain product's availability in a given market, and if the related performance measure was the overall market share of that product, we determined that the two were not aligned. Further, if a performance measure attempted to measure something beyond the control of the participant to effectively influence, we did not consider the measure and constraint to be aligned. We determined that 4 percent of the performance measures were either not applicable or not categorizable. See appendix I for a full description of our scope and methodology.

GAO-13-740 Agricultural Trade

is better able to assess whether the participant's performance is meeting expectations.

5. **Performance measure has associated baselines.** FAS guidelines state that each performance measure should have an associated baseline. We found that 359 of the 375 measures in our sample (96 percent) had associated baselines, indicating that they were based on an initial market review and that the performance measures were consistent from year to year. However, we also found that the baselines did not appear to inform the goals for subsequent years. For example, one participant had a baseline of 105 buyer/seller introductions but set a goal of 35 for the following year. The result for that year—164—not only exceeded the baseline but also exceeded the goal by more than 468 percent, calling into question whether the baseline was appropriate for the performance measure.[43]

6. **Performance measure has an identified methodology**. FAS guidelines for reviewing country progress reports state that the reports must identify the methodologies used to assess results for each performance measure. The reports that we reviewed identified a methodology—that is, an information source, an approach for assessing results, or both—for 224 of the 373 performance measures (60 percent). For example, one progress report identified "[r]esults gathered from consumer surveys during in-store promotions" as the information source and the approach used to assess results of activities intended to increase consumer awareness. Another report identified the information source and the approach as "2009 results based on 334 informal customer surveys conducted throughout the year" and explained how certain results were averaged to provide aggregated numbers. For the 149 performance measures with no identified methodology (40 percent), it would be difficult for FAS to determine the reliability of the reported results.[44]

Table 6 summarizes the results of our analysis of the sample of country progress reports that we reviewed.

---

[43]An FAS official told us that this participant lacked a clear methodology to break the target data down from worldwide to specific markets, and they therefore understated it in this particular market for 2008. FAS continued to work with the participant and, according to FAS officials, the data are much more accurate for the most current reporting year.

[44]We did not evaluate the methodologies' quality or reliability.

Table 6: Summary of GAO Analysis of Sampled Country Progress Reports

Criterion	Met criterion[a]
Constraint or opportunity has at least one outcome measure.	105 of 115 constraints or opportunities
Performance measure is clear.	356 of 378 performance measures
Performance measure is aligned with related constraint or opportunity.	330 of 378 performance measures
Performance measure is quantifiable.	378 of 378 performance measures
Performance measure has associated baseline.	359 of 375 performance measures
Performance measure has an identified methodology.	224 of 373 performance measures

Source: GAO and USDA Foreign Agriculture Service.

[a]Denominators vary because certain criteria were not applicable to some performance measures.

In addition, a comparison of participants' measurable goals and reported results in the progress reports that we reviewed showed that those participants met or exceeded a combined total of 222 of 357 (62 percent) of their goals. However, the extent to which participants met the goals varied widely; some participants exceeded a goal by more than 1,000 percent, while others attained less than 10 percent of the goal. FAS guidance requires that participants monitor their progress relative to their stated goals but has not established requirements for whether, when, or how participants should meet their goals. According to FAS officials, narratives in the progress reports should address whether and why actual results did or did not meet goals and what changes are needed to address any disparities. FAS officials noted that if an FAS marketing specialist reviewing a funding application notices wide discrepancies between the participant's goals and results for the previous year, the specialist will collaborate with the participant to identify lessons that can be learned and will look for corresponding changes in the participant's strategy for the coming year.

FAS Requires MAP and FMD Participants to Conduct Comprehensive Evaluations When Appropriate

FAS requires that program participants conduct evaluations of their program activities when appropriate or required by FAS. Current MAP regulation defines a program evaluation as a review of the participant's entire program or an appropriate portion of the program as agreed to by the participant and FAS.[45] These reviews can range from external, third-party evaluations, such as cost-benefit analyses, to participants' internal reevaluations of their approaches to market development activities. FAS officials reported that they received a combined total of 71 third-party program evaluations from 43 participants in 2010 and 2011.[46] Additionally, eight of 10 U.S. agricultural export promotion groups surveyed by an industry contractor reported that they conducted country, regional, or global evaluations during the last 3 years.

Because the program evaluations are conducted on a case-by-case basis and may cover only a portion of a participant's market development activities (e.g., market development efforts in 1 of 20 countries where a participant conducts its activities), it is difficult to determine what portion of all market development efforts are assessed through these evaluations. One FAS contractor who had previously conducted third-party evaluations for MAP and FMD participants told us that factors such as the size of the participants and the value the participant places on monitoring and evaluation affected the frequency, depth, and usefulness of evaluations that his firm had conducted.[47]

---

[45]7 C.F.R. § 1485.23.

[46]The 43 participants that provided evaluations in 2010 and 2011 included 13 of the participants that provided the country progress reports in our random sample. We did not assess the quality of the evaluations, because such an assessment was beyond the scope of this engagement.

[47]FAS officials noted that mandating a program-wide fixed frequency for evaluations would be overly inflexible and not always practical, since participants' award amounts range in size from tens of thousands to tens of millions of dollars.

FAS Cost-Benefit Analysis Asserts That MAP and FMD Benefit U.S. Economy, but Methodological Limitations May Affect the Magnitude of Estimated Benefits

A 2007 cost-benefit analysis of MAP and FMD, commissioned by FAS, found that the programs increased U.S. agricultural exports and benefitted the U.S. economy.[48] Overall, the study asserted that the government's expenditures for the two programs had resulted in greater increases in U.S. agricultural exports and greater benefit to the U.S. economy than would have occurred without the expenditures. However, the study's two econometric models estimating the programs' benefits have methodological limitations that may affect the accuracy of the estimates. First, the model used to estimate changes in market share omitted important variables, and, second, a sensitivity analysis of key assumptions was not conducted for that and another model that the study used. FAS officials reported that they plan to commission a new cost-benefit analysis in 2014 but indicated that they have not yet identified the methodologies that the new analysis will use.

FAS-Commissioned Cost-Benefit Analysis Asserted Benefits of Market Development Programs

The 2007 cost-benefit analysis, conducted by Global Insight, Inc., found that MAP and FMD had positive effects on agricultural export activities. The study also asserted that without public-sector funding, the private sector would under invest in agricultural market development, negatively affecting the U.S. economy—an outcome known as market failure.[49] The study used data from fiscal years 2002 through 2006 to estimate the economic effects of FAS's program expenditures under the 2002 farm bill

---

[48]Global Insight, Inc., *Cost-Benefit Analysis of USDA's Export Market Development Programs*, 2007. In 2010, FAS commissioned Global Insight to perform an updated analysis, using data for 2002 through 2008 (IHS Global Insight [USA], Inc., "A Cost-Benefit Analysis of USDA's International Market Development Programs," March 2010). The 2010 update's conclusions are similar to those of the 2007 study; however, the 2010 update does not include an explanation of its results and methodology and instead refers to this information in the 2007 study. For that reason, we focused our review on the 2007 study.

[49]The 2007 study asserts that several types of market failure would, absent U.S. government funding for agricultural market development, cause the private sector to under invest in market development and have negative impacts on the U.S. economy. A market failure is commonly defined as a situation in which an unregulated competitive market is inefficient, because prices fail to provide proper signals to consumers and producers. In the presence of a market failure, the government can intervene and provide policy through regulation, taxes, or subsidies to bring the market to equilibrium. See appendix IV for more information.

and of FAS's possible expenditures under a hypothetical 2007 farm bill.[50] Following are key estimates from the 2007 study.

- The study estimated that the increased market promotion and development funding authorized for MAP and FMD in the 2002 farm bill—almost doubling from roughly $125 million in fiscal year 2001, before the bill's enactment, to approximately $234 million in fiscal year 2006—raised the U.S. share of global agricultural exports from 18 percent to 19 percent, equivalent to a $3.8 billion increase in trade. The study estimated that as a result, economic welfare increased by $828 million.[51]

- The study estimated that if annual MAP and FMD spending under the hypothetical 2007 farm bill in fiscal years 2007 through 2015 were equivalent to spending under the 2002 farm bill in fiscal year 2006, the U.S. share of global agricultural exports would rise from 19 percent in 2007 to 20.9 percent in 2015—equal to $84 billion in U.S. exports in 2015. If spending under the hypothetical 2007 farm bill increased by 50 percent over the 2006 level, U.S. exports would increase to $86.4 billion in 2015 and economic welfare would increase by $740 million. On the other hand, the study suggested that if the hypothetical bill did not authorize funding for the two programs, U.S. exports would grow to $75.5 billion by 2015 and economic welfare would decrease by $1.1 billion.

- The study found that market development promotions for certain U.S. high-value commodities have a positive effect—known as a spillover effect—on exports of other U.S. high-value commodities.[52]

- The study estimated that every dollar spent for agricultural market development under the 2002 farm bill increased economic welfare by $5.20; under the hypothetical 2007 bill, every dollar would increase

---

[50]See the Farm Security and Rural Investment Act of 2002, Pub. L. No. 107-17, 116 Stat. 134 (commonly referred to as the 2002 Farm Bill). Typically, the farm bill is reauthorized every 5 years. At the time of the 2007 Global Insight study, the 2002 bill had not yet been reauthorized. As a result, the study postulated a hypothetical 2007 farm bill under three different scenarios.

[51]Economic welfare can be defined as the well-being of society due to the production and consumption of goods and services.

[52]The 2007 study refers to the spillover effect as a "halo effect."

economic welfare by $4.10. In contrast, eliminating the funding would reduce economic welfare by $4.30 per eliminated dollar, resulting in a $1.1 billion loss to the U.S. economy.

Economic Models Used to Estimate MAP's and FMD's Benefits Have Limitations That May Affect Estimates' Accuracy

Two models that Global Insight used to estimate the effects of MAP and FMD on the U.S. economy have methodological limitations that may affect the models' ability to accurately estimate the programs' benefits to the U.S. economy. As with any study using economic models, the lack of data forces researchers to make certain assumptions, and the resulting estimates are affected by the methodologies chosen and the assumptions used. In general, the 2007 study assumes that FAS program expenditures lead to an increase in private-sector expenditures. To estimate the economic effects of the program assistance, the 2007 study employed two economic models commonly used in cost-benefit analysis: (1) A market share model to estimate the effect of expenditures under the 2002 farm bill and the hypothetical 2007 farm bill on the U.S. agricultural market share of global markets and (2) a spillover effect model to estimate increases in U.S. agricultural exports due to promotions of other U.S. exported commodities.[53] However, these models have limitations that may affect their ability to accurately estimate the economic benefits of MAP and FMD. FAS officials reported that they plan to commission a new cost-benefit analysis in fiscal year 2014, but they indicated that they have not yet identified the methodologies that the new study will use.

Market Share Model

To examine the effect of the 2002 farm bill and the potential effect of the hypothetical 2007 farm bill, the 2007 study used a U.S. market share model to simulate the market share for U.S. high-value and bulk commodities in global markets from 1975 through 2004.[54] However, the model has limitations related to its exclusion of important variables and its lack of a sensitivity analysis of key assumptions.

---

[53]The 2007 study uses a computable general equilibrium model to analyze the impact of MAP and FMD on the larger farm economy and other segments of the U.S. economy. See appendix V for a description of this analysis.

[54]According to the study, USDA classification for bulk commodities includes wheat, soybeans, cotton, and other commodities while high-value products include wine and beer, snack foods, red meat, fresh or processed fruits and vegetables, nursery products, and other processed, ready-to-eat products.

Excluded Variables

The 2007 study's use of the market share model controlled for four variables across each year: (1) the U.S. market share in the previous year, (2) the currency exchange rate, (3) combined FAS program expenditures and participants' contributions over time,[55] and (4) a time trend to account for any omitted variables. However, the model excludes some variables that could be important for determining the U.S. market share—in particular, industry-specific variables such as commodity prices, production volumes, and number of export competitors.[56] Although the study states that a linear trend variable is included as a proxy for missing variables in the model, this variable cannot be expected to capture the full effects of such industry-specific variables. By limiting the model to the four variables, the study may bias the effect of these variables by incorrectly identifying the magnitude of these variables and the statistical significance of their effect on U.S. market shares.

Lack of Sensitivity Analysis

The 2007 study used the market share model to examine the possible effects of the hypothetical 2007 farm bill under three scenarios.[57]

---

[55]By combining FAS and participant expenditures, the market share model in the 2007 study estimated the effect of total expenditures on U.S. market shares, in contrast with models found in the literature. As a result, it is not possible to separate or compare the effect of FAS expenditures versus private sector expenditures of marketing programs on U.S. exports.

[56]This limitation is known as omitted variable bias.

[57]In addition to estimating the hypothetical 2007 farm bill's effects on U.S. agricultural exports, the 2007 study used the market share model to examine the 2002 farm bill's effects on U.S. exports from 2002 through 2020 under two scenarios. The first scenario involved actual FAS program expenditures set by the 2002 farm bill that gradually increased over a 5-year period and actual participant promotion expenditures that also increased over time. The second scenario assumed constant FAS program expenditures and participant expenditures that were set at the fiscal year 2001 levels. Both scenarios assumed that the FAS program expenditures and participant expenditures would revert to the 2001 levels after 2007. After comparing the two scenarios, the study concluded that every dollar of FAS program expenditure had a return of $25 in agricultural export gains. The study further estimated that, absent increased FAS funding for the two market development programs, households would need to be compensated by a total $828 million by 2020 because of the loss of U.S. exports.

GAO-13-740 Agricultural Trade

1. The first scenario assumed that FAS program expenditures and participant contributions would remain constant. On the basis of these assumptions, the study predicted that U.S. exports would increase from $65 billion in 2006 to $84 billion in 2015.

2. The second scenario assumed that FAS would increase program expenditures and that participants would increase their contributions gradually, spending 50 percent more by 2012 than in 2007. On the basis of these assumptions, the study predicted that U.S. exports would increase from $65 billion in 2006 to about $86 billion in 2015.

3. The third scenario assumed that FAS would immediately eliminate program expenditures in 2008 and that, as a result, participants would spend less of their own resources on market development, gradually decreasing their spending by 50 percent by 2012 compared with 2007. On the basis of these assumptions, the study predicted that U.S. exports would increase from $65 billion in 2006 to $75.5 billion in 2015.

Following Office of Management and Budget guidelines for conducting a cost-benefit analysis,[58] the study included a sensitivity analysis of the market share model's predictions, assessing the level of confidence in the predictions with a 95 percent confidence interval.[59] However, the study did not include a sensitivity analysis of the third scenario's assumption regarding participants' response to the elimination of FAS funding.[60] In particular, the study did not examine the effects that a range of participants' responses to the elimination of FAS funding would have on the U.S. market share. That is, the study did not consider whether participants' market development spending would remain constant, would decrease at lower rates than the 50 percent that the study assumed, or would increase to the level of the eliminated FAS expenditures. Best practices for cost estimation dictate the inclusion of a sensitivity analysis

---

[58]Office of Management and Budget, Circular A-94, "Guidelines and Discount Rates for Benefit-Cost Analysis of Federal Programs" (Oct. 29, 1992), accessed July 15, 2013, http://www.whitehouse.gov/omb/circulars_a094.

[59]With an average prediction error of less than 5 percent, the study concluded that the market share model was a good fit for the data used.

[60]The 2007 study also did not conduct a sensitivity analysis of the second scenarios' assumption that FAS expenditures and participant contributions would both increase by 50 percent by 2012.

to ascertain the effect of the assumption on the results.[61] For a sensitivity analysis to reveal the effect of a changed assumption on a cost estimate, the analysis must examine the effect of changing one assumption while holding all other assumptions and variables constant. In addition, the study did not provide any insight or data to support the assumption that participants would reduce their spending if FAS program funding were eliminated.

Spillover Effect Model

The 2007 study used a spillover effect model to test the assumption that increasing the market promotion of one U.S. commodity has a positive effect on exports of other U.S. commodities. The study found that the effects of the relationships between commodity promotions and exports ranged from positive to negative and varied in magnitude but that, overall, the positive effects outweighed the negative effects. The model examined the relationship between U.S. market promotions and exports for four high-value products—almonds, apples, grapes, and wine—for the period 1985 through 2004.[62] For example, increased U.S. promotion of almonds led to increased U.S. exports of grapes but to decreased exports of wine and had no effect on apple exports. Conversely, increased U.S. promotion of grapes led to decreased U.S. exports of almonds but to increased exports of apples and wine.[63]

Although the study estimated the size of the spillover effect, it did not include a sensitivity analysis of a key assumption used for this estimate. The study assumed that some type of market development as a result of U.S. market promotions occurs in 64 percent of all markets for U.S.

---

[61]GAO, *GAO Cost Estimating and Assessment Guide: Best Practices for Developing and Managing Capital Program Costs*, GAO-09-3SP (Washington, D.C.: Mar. 2, 2009).

[62]The study did not explain why the spillover effect model excluded bulk commodities from the analysis.

[63]According to Office of Management and Budget officials, the spillover effect differs from a multiplier effect and should be considered a positive externality. Moreover, the spillover effect differs from the multiplier effect in that no increased income from other industries causes them to increase their purchases of other items. For example, increase in demand abroad for U.S. wines is a direct effect of market promotion, but it is a positive externality if that promotion results in higher demand for other agricultural products. The spillover effect occurs if the promotion of U.S. wine causes consumers' improved perceptions of wine to increase their desire to buy U.S. apples.

exports.[64] To estimate the spillover effect of FAS market promotions, the model used this assumption, unsupported by data or industry evidence, as well as the estimated effects of promotions of one commodity on the exported quantities of other commodities.[65] According to the study, the spillover effect of FAS market promotions ranges from 24 percent to 54 percent of the total growth in overall market development. However, the study did not include a sensitivity analysis of the effect of changing the assumption that development occurs in 64 percent of markets as a result of U.S. market promotions. That is, the study did not examine the extent to which assuming a higher or lower percentage of market development would change the magnitude of the estimated spillover effect.

Conclusions

For many years, MAP and FMD—the two programs that receive most of USDA's market development funding—have provided continuing assistance to an established pool of agricultural trade associations, primarily to promote generic commodities overseas. FAS has developed a performance monitoring framework in which FMD and MAP participants are expected to develop measurable objectives—that is, constraints and opportunities—linked to performance measures that allow them to annually compare their results with established baselines and goals. Participants generally followed this framework successfully; however, many of the participants' annual country progress reports that we reviewed did not identify, as FAS guidelines require, the methodologies used to assess results for each performance measure. These gaps limit FAS's ability to determine the reliability of program results reported by participants and to accurately assess participants' progress and success in achieving program objectives.

The 2007 cost-benefit analysis that FAS commissioned asserted that MAP and FMD have increased U.S. exports and benefited the U.S. economy. However, one econometric model that the study used to

---

[64]The study based this assumption on an assumption that U.S. market promotions result in some type of market development in 80 percent of the U.S. export markets for 80 percent of U.S. products. The study did not state whether the U.S. export markets were strictly U.S. agricultural export markets or export markets for all U.S. products. In addition, the study did not define "market development," which could include increased consumer awareness, increased exports, or increased promotional events and materials, among other effects.

[65]The study referred to this effect as cross-promotion elasticity.

estimate the programs' effects excluded variables that have significant impact on U.S. market shares. As a result, the model may bias the estimates of the variables that it included. In addition, because another model that the study used did not include a sensitivity analysis of certain assumptions, it is not possible to determine the degree to which those assumptions would affect the model's results. For example, one scenario assumed that if FAS suddenly eliminated all MAP and FMD expenditures, participants would reduce their own spending on market development by 50 percent. However, the study does not examine the effects of participants' other possible responses to the elimination of FAS expenditures, such as maintaining their spending or increasing it to compensate for the eliminated FAS funds. Accurate cost benefit analyses help decision makers determine how best to allocate program funding and provide a better picture of the potential effect on U.S. exports and the economy if funding is increased or decreased.

Recommendations for Executive Action

We recommend that the Secretary of Agriculture direct FAS to take the following three actions:

To improve MAP and FMD participants' annual reporting of the results of their market development activities,

- use appropriate means to emphasize the importance of participants' identifying the methodologies used to assess results for each performance measure in their annual country progress reports.

To improve the accuracy of future cost-benefit analyses of FAS's market development programs,

- ensure that any econometric model used for the cost-benefit analysis, such as the market share model, includes industry-specific variables that could have a significant role in determining the U.S. market share—for example, commodity prices, production volumes, and number of export competitors; and

- conduct a sensitivity analysis, in accordance with best practices for cost estimates, of the key assumptions that are applied in any economic models used in the cost-benefit analysis, such as the market share model and spillover effect model.

Agency Comments

USDA provided written comments about a draft version of this report, concurring with our findings and recommendations (see app. VI for a copy of these comments). USDA also provided technical comments, which we incorporated as appropriate.

As agreed with your office, we plan no further distribution until 30 days from the report date. At that time, we will send a copy to USDA. In addition, the report will be available at no charge on the GAO website at http://www.gao.gov.

If you or your staff have any questions about this report, please contact me at (202) 512-4802 or evansl@gao.gov. Contact points for our Offices of Congressional Relations and Public Affairs may be found on the last page of this report. GAO staff who made significant contributions to this report are listed in appendix VII.

Sincerely yours,

Lawrance Evans Jr.
Director, International Affairs and Trade

Appendix I: Objectives, Scope, and Methodology

We were asked to review several aspects of the U.S. Department of Agriculture's (USDA) five market development programs, which USDA's Foreign Agriculture Service (FAS) administers. This report (1) describes participation and expenditures in these market development programs, particularly the Market Access Program (MAP) and Foreign Market Development Program (FMD); (2) examines FAS's management and monitoring of its market development programs; and (3) assesses FAS's cost-benefit analysis of MAP's and FMD's impact on the U.S. economy. Because MAP and FMD receive most of USDA's market development funding, we focused our review primarily on program participation in those two programs.

For our first and second objectives, we selected five program participants as case studies: the American Hardwood Export Council, the California Table Grape Commission, the Wine Institute, Cotton Council International, and the Western United States Agricultural Trade Association. To select the four commodity group participants, we examined market development program expenditure data for 2002 through 2011. We chose participants that used more than one market development program and had spent a significant amount of their market development funds in the two countries—Japan and Mexico—that we selected for our review. The four groups consisted of at least one bulk commodity group, one nonfood commodity group, and one high-value commodity group, and one horticultural group. All four were MAP participants, and two were also FMD participants. In addition, we included one of four state regional trade groups in our sample, because these groups allocate the majority of MAP funds to small businesses for branded product promotion. We reviewed additional documents, including agreement letters, strategic plans, country progress reports, program evaluations, and other information provided by FAS and the participants. We also interviewed U.S.-based headquarters staff from each of the five organizations. Additionally, we conducted fieldwork in Japan and Mexico, interviewing FAS staff in the Agricultural Trade Offices in Tokyo, Osaka, and Mexico City, as well as representatives of program participants in each country. We also observed several trade promotion activities and visited retailers where U.S. products were sold. We selected Japan and Mexico because they are in different geographic regions and are among the countries where program participants have spent the largest shares of USDA market development funds. In addition, for all of three of our objectives, we interviewed FAS staff in headquarters, contractors that FAS uses for aspects of its market promotion programs, and subject matter experts in the field of trade economics. We also reviewed relevant laws, regulations, and FAS guidelines.

To describe agricultural groups' participation in FAS's five market development programs and the programs' expenditures from 2002 through 2011—our first objective—we reviewed program participants' applications, country progress reports, and program evaluations to identify examples of the activities that participants undertook with market development funding. We also analyzed expenditure data for the five programs from 2002 through 2011 to understand the nature of program participation and to identify program participants with the largest expenditures as well as changes in participants' expenditures. We reviewed MAP and FMD expenditure data by country to determine where participants spent the largest amounts of program funding. Further, we compared participants' matching contributions with their expenditure levels to determine whether participants were meeting program cost-sharing requirements. In addition, we reviewed expenditure data for the MAP branded products program for 2002 through 2011 to determine the scope of the branded products program, including the number of small businesses participating and the number affected by the 5-year graduation requirement. To assess the reliability of market development program expenditure and contribution data that FAS provided, we conducted electronic and manual data testing and held interviews with knowledgeable USDA staff members. On the basis of our assessment of the data and our interviews with the staff members, the data appear to be reliable for the purposes of this report.

To examine FAS's management and monitoring of the market development programs—part of our second objective—we discussed management practices and the use of the Unified Export Strategy (UES) system, which participants use to apply for multiple programs to reduce risks of overlap and duplication among the five programs with FAS officials. We also met with FAS's Compliance Review Branch to review FAS's process for verifying participants' expenditures and contributions for all programs in which they participated. In addition, to verify that small businesses participating in the MAP branded products program did not receive MAP funds from more than one MAP participant for promotion in the same country, we reviewed expenditure data for the MAP branded products program for 2011.[1] We examined all businesses that had spent MAP funds, the countries where they spent the funds, and the MAP

---

[1] According to FAS, small businesses should not obtain MAP funds from more than one MAP participant to promote the same brand name product in the same country. They may use funds from a second MAP participant to promote a product in a different country.

participants that allocated these funds to the businesses through the
branded products program. We identified, and reviewed with FAS, any
instances in which a business may have spent in a single country funds
received from two MAP participants.

To determine whether MAP and FMD participants were assessing results
in accordance with FAS performance monitoring guidelines—also part of
our second objective—we developed an assessment tool to analyze a
sample of participants' annual country progress reports. We selected a
random but nongeneralizable sample of 20 participants in MAP and FMD,
and we identified countries where these participants spent more than
$5,000 in 3 consecutive fiscal years, 2008 through 2010. We requested
the country progress reports for all 20 participants for each of the 3
years—a total of 60 progress reports. After requesting the 60 reports, we
removed four groups on being informed that those groups use other
forms of reporting; we also removed two state regional trade groups. After
we requested additional randomly selected progress reports, our final
sample totaled 56 reports. Where progress reports covered a region
rather than a specific country, we used regional data and country-specific
data as available. We selected criteria, based on FAS guidelines for
developing the progress reports[2] and key attributes of successful
performance measurement that we previously identified,[3] to assess
constraints and performance measures in the reports that we reviewed.
These criteria are as follows: (1) each constraint has at least one
outcome measure; (2) the performance measure is clear; (3) the
performance measure is aligned with the related constraint or opportunity;
(4) the performance measure is quantifiable; (5) the performance
measure has an associated baseline; and (6) the performance measure
has an identified methodology. We also compared the goals and results
reported for each performance measure to determine the extent to which
the goals were met and the results were reported. We recorded each
constraint and performance measure from the country progress reports
we reviewed, and two reviewers coded separate analyses for each
criterion. The two analyses were then reconciled to produce a final result.
In addition, we requested from FAS all third-party program evaluations

---

[2]Agralytica, *Results-Oriented Management: A Guide for FAS Industry Partners* (Arlington,
Va.: 2001).

[3]GAO, *Tax Administration: IRS Needs to Further Refine Its Tax Filing Season
Performance Measures*, GAO-03-143 (Washington, D.C.: Nov. 22, 2002).

associated with our random sample of participants and countries in the 3-year timeframe. FAS informed us that the evaluations were too difficult to identify using these parameters and provided a list of 71 evaluations that 43 participants, including 13 of those in our sample, submitted in 2010 and 2011. We did not assess the quality of the evaluations, because such an assessment was beyond the scope of this engagement.

To assess FAS's cost-benefit analysis of MAP's and FMD's impact on the U.S. economy—our third objective—we analyzed studies of MAP and FMD commissioned by FAS and published in 2007 and 2010, respectively, by Global Insight, Inc.[4] We conducted structured interviews with the studies' authors, agency officials, and academics involved in the studies. We also reviewed relevant research on market development programs. In addition, we reviewed Office of Management and Budget guidelines for conducting cost-benefit analyses and interviewed office officials.[5] We evaluated the studies on the basis of GAO's cost estimation guide,[6] prior related GAO work,[7] and internal expertise.

We conducted this performance audit from August 2012 to July 2013 in accordance with generally accepted government auditing standards. Those standards require that we plan and perform the audit to obtain sufficient, appropriate evidence to provide a reasonable basis for our findings and conclusions based on our audit objectives. We believe that the evidence obtained provides a reasonable basis for our findings and conclusions based on our audit objectives.

---

[4]Global Insight, Inc., *Cost-Benefit Analysis of USDA's Export Market Development Programs*, 2007. IHS Global Insight (USA), Inc., "A Cost-Benefit Analysis of USDA's International Market Development Programs," March 2010.

[5]Office of Management and Budget, Circular A-94, "Guidelines and Discount Rates for Benefit-Cost Analysis of Federal Programs" (Oct. 29, 1992), accessed July 15, 2013, http://www.whitehouse.gov/omb/circulars_a094.

[6]GAO, *GAO Cost Estimating and Assessment Guide: Best Practices for Developing and Managing Capital Program Costs*, GAO-09-3SP (Washington, D.C.: Mar. 2, 2009).

[7]GAO, *Agricultural Trade: Changes Made to Market Access Program, but Questions Remain on Economic Impact*, NSIAD-99-38 (Washington, D.C.: Apr. 5, 1999).

Appendix II: USDA Market Development Program Recipients and Award Amounts in Fiscal Year 2012

Many organizations participate in more than one of the five U.S. Department of Agriculture (USDA) market development programs. FAS allocates the majority of USDA's market development funding for the Market Access Program (MAP), which has the largest number of participants. Table 7 shows the 103 program participants and their award amounts in fiscal year 2012, in descending order of total award amounts. The table does not show small businesses that received a share of MAP funding indirectly for branded product promotion.

Table 7: Market Development Program Participants and Total Awards in Fiscal Year 2012, in Descending Order of Total Award Amounts

Dollars in thousands

	Participants	MAP	FMD	EMP	TASC	QSP	Total
1	Cotton Council International	$18,954	$4,177				**$23,131**
2	U.S. Meat Export Federation	$19,704	$1,427				**$21,131**
3	AHEC, APA, SEC, SFPA[a]	$9,116	$2,548				**$11,664**
4	U.S. Wheat Associates	$6,093	$5,150	$338		$46	**$11,627**
5	U.S. Grains Council	$7,341	$3,877	$261			**$11,479**
6	Food Export Association of the Midwest USA	$11,195					**$11,195**
7	Western United States Agricultural Trade Association	$9,970					**$9,970**
8	American Soybean Association	$3,562	$5,392	$501			**$9,455**
9	Food Export USA Northeast	$9,362					**$9,362**
10	Wine Institute	$6,938					**$6,938**
11	USA Poultry and Egg Export Council	$5,001	$1,266	$209			**$6,476**
12	National Potato Promotion Board	$4,767		$335	$45	$460	**$5,607**
13	Southern United States Trade Association	$4,818		$199			**$5,017**
14	U.S. Dairy Export Council	$4,161	$554	$120			**$4,835**
15	Florida Department of Citrus	$4,590					**$4,590**
16	Washington Apple Commission	$4,509					**$4,509**
17	USA Rice Federation/U.S. Rice Producers Association	$2,785	$1,532	$106			**$4,423**
18	California Walnut Commission	$4,164				$75	**$4,239**
19	Alaska Seafood Marketing Institute	$4,076					**$4,076**
20	Foreign Agricultural Service, USDA (multiple projects)			$3,734			**$3,734**
21	Blue Diamond Growers/Almond Board of California	$3,354	$300		$35		**$3,689**
22	California Table Grape Commission	$3,506					**$3,506**
23	American Peanut Council	$2,361	$603	$82			**$3,046**
24	Pear Bureau Northwest	$2,866		$113			**$2,979**
25	Raisin Administrative Committee	$2,493					**$2,493**

Dollars in thousands

Participants		MAP	FMD	EMP	TASC	QSP	Total
26	Sunkist Growers, Inc.	$2,232					**$2,232**
27	California Prune Board	$2,209					**$2,209**
28	Cranberry Marketing Committee	$1,514	$200		$384	$24	**$2,122**
29	U.S. Livestock Genetics Exports, Inc.	$1,000	$607	$87		$174	**$1,867**
30	National Renderers Association	$813	$801				**$1,614**
31	Washington State Fruit Commission	$1,551					**$1,551**
32	National Sunflower Association	$1,163	$254				**$1,418**
33	U.S. Dry Bean Council	$1,130	$109	$168			**$1,406**
34	Pet Food Institute	$1,345					**$1,345**
35	National Confectioners Association	$1,335					**$1,335**
36	Bryant Christie, Inc.				$1,295		**$1,295**
37	U.S. Apple Export Council	$963			$223		**$1,186**
38	USA Dry Pea and Lentil Council	$806	$166	$154		$14	**$1,140**
39	National Association of State Departments of Agriculture	$1,091					**$1,091**
40	Welch Foods, Inc.	$845		$83			**$928**
41	California Strawberry Commission	$920					**$920**
42	Northwest Wine Promotion Coalition	$872					**$872**
43	Cal-Pure Pistachios/Western Pistachio Association	$845					**$845**
44	Ginseng Board of Wisconsin	$200			$348	$225	**$774**
45	Intertribal Agriculture Council	$706					**$706**
46	American Sheep Industry Association	$175	$156			$320	**$652**
47	California Agricultural Export Council	$318				$300	**$618**
48	California Cherry Advisory Board	$608					**$608**
49	Chapman University				$565		**$565**
50	Idaho Potato Commission/ Idaho State Department of Agriculture				$540		**$540**
51	Cooperative Resources International			$531			**$531**
52	California Strawberry Nurserymen's Association				$520		**$520**
53	California Cherry Marketing and Research Board				$502		**$502**
54	California Citrus Mutual				$500		**$500**
55	California Cling Peach Board	$447					**$447**
56	Organic Trade Association	$435					**$435**
57	New York Wine and Grape Foundation	$408					**$408**
58	Brewers Association Inc.	$401					**$401**
59	American Biomass Trade Cooperative	$157			$200		**$357**
60	World Wide Sires, Ltd.			$354			**$354**

Dollars in thousands

Participants		MAP	FMD	EMP	TASC	QSP	Total
61	The Popcorn Board	$344					**$344**
62	Synergistic Hawaii Agriculture Council				$330		**$330**
63	Napa Valley Vintners			$311			**$311**
64	Distilled Spirits Council	$258		$45			**$303**
65	California Pear Advisory Board	$265		$25			**$290**
66	American Seed Trade Association	$84	$203				**$287**
67	Mohair Council of America	$32	$16			$235	**$283**
68	The Catfish Institute	$280					**$280**
69	National Pecan Growers Council	$271					**$271**
70	Oregon Department of Agriculture				$271		**$271**
71	Alaska Agricultural Development and Marketing			$268			**$268**
72	California Fresh Tomato Growers/Florida Tomato Committee	$265					**$265**
73	Cherry Marketing Institute	$204		$30		$30	**$264**
74	JBC International, Inc.			$255			**$255**
75	National Watermelon Promotion Board	$245					**$245**
76	International Food Information Council Foundation			$241			**$241**
77	U.S. Hide, Skin & Leather Association	$77	$90	$60			**$226**
78	Citrus Research Board				$222		**$222**
79	U.S. Hop Plant Protection Committee				$212		**$212**
80	Agricultural Research Service, USDA			$210			**$210**
81	Hawaii Papaya Industry Association	$198					**$198**
82	University of Alaska				$181		**$181**
83	Hop Growers of America	$175				$5	**$180**
84	Leather Industries of America		$159				**$159**
85	California Table Grape Export Association				$153		**$153**
86	American Pistachio Growers/Cal-Pure Pistachios Inc.			$150			**$150**
87	University of Maryland			$132			**$132**
88	Minnesota Department of Agriculture			$108			**$108**
89	Promar Consulting			$106			**$106**
90	Texas Produce Export Association	$98					**$98**
91	California Grape & Tree Fruit League				$97		**$97**
92	International Center for Aquaculture and Aquatic Environments, Auburn University			$85			**$85**
93	North Carolina State University				$84		**$84**
94	National Hay Association	$17	$47				**$64**
95	Independent Grocers Alliance Institute, Inc.			$64			**$64**

Dollars in thousands

Participants		MAP	FMD	EMP	TASC	QSP	Total
96	North American Millers Association		$58				**$58**
97	World Food Logistics			$57			**$57**
98	Minor Crop Farmer Alliance				$34		**$34**
99	Animal and Plant Health Inspection Service, USDA				$25		**$25**
100	Potato Variety Management Institute			$22			**$22**
101	Northwest Horticultural Council				$22		**$22**
102	Western Growers				$14		**$14**
103	Economic Research Service, USDA			$14			**$14**
Total		**$182,989**	**$29,693**	**$9,556**	**$6,803**	**$1,908**	**$230,949**

Source: GAO analysis of USDA data.

Notes:

Numbers in columns and rows may not sum to totals because of rounding.

Some participants in the Emerging Markets Program (EMP), Quality Samples Program (QSP), and Technical Assistance for Specialty Crops Program (TASC) received multiple awards for specific projects. In those instances, the sum of each participant's awards for each program is shown.

MAP = Market Access Program

FMD = Foreign Market Development Program

EMP = Emerging Markets Program

QSP = Quality Samples Program

TASC = Technical Assistance for Specialty Crops Program

[a]The American Hardwood Export Council (AHEC), the Engineered Wood Association (APA), the Softwood Export Council (SEC), and the Southern Forest Products Association (SFPA) collectively submit single applications for MAP and FMD awards.

Appendix III: Expenditures in 2011 for the Emerging Markets Program, Quality Samples Program, and Technical Assistance for Specialty Crops Program

Tables 8 through 10 show USDA market development program participants that spent the largest amounts of funds provided by the Emerging Markets Program (EMP), Quality Samples Program (QSP), and Technical Assistance for Specialty Crops Program (TASC) funds in 2011. Table 11 shows the countries where the largest amounts of funding for the three programs were spent in 2011.

Table 8: Program Participants with Largest Expenditures for Emerging Markets Program (EMP) in 2011

Dollars in thousands

Participant ranking by expenditure amount		EMP expenditures
1	World Wide Sires	$819
2	USA Poultry and Egg Export Council	362
3	American Soybean Association	253
4	U.S. Wheat Associates	170
5	U.S. Dry Bean Council	155
6	American Legend Cooperative	130
7	California Milk Advisory Board	126
8	Texas Tech University	106
9	University of Georgia	102
10	Pear Bureau Northwest	87
Participants' total EMP expenditures		**$2,309**
(percentage of all EMP participants' expenditures)		**(79%)**
All EMP participants' expenditures		**$2,906**

Source: GAO analysis of USDA data.

Notes:

Twenty-five organizations expended EMP funds in 2011.

Numbers in columns may not sum to totals because of rounding.

Data shown are as of September 25, 2012.

Appendix III: Expenditures in 2011 for the
Emerging Markets Program, Quality Samples
Program, and Technical Assistance for
Specialty Crops Program

Table 9: Program Participants with Largest Expenditures for Quality Samples Program (QSP) in 2011

Dollars in thousands

Participant ranking by expenditure amount		QSP expenditures
1	California Agricultural Export Council	$345
2	National Potato Promotion Board	157
3	National Pecan Growers Council	75
4	U.S. Livestock Genetics Export, Inc.	60
5	U.S. Wheat Associates	53
6	Mohair Council of America	35
7	California Walnut Commission	25
8	American Soybean Association	22
9	California Milk Advisory Board	15
10	Alaska Seafood Marketing Institute	15
Participants' total expenditures		**$802**
(percentage of all QSP participants' expenditures)		**(96%)**
All QSP participants' expenditures		**$839**

Source: GAO analysis of USDA data.

Notes:

Fifteen organizations expended QSP funds in 2011.

Numbers in columns may not sum to totals because of rounding.

Data shown are as of September 25, 2012.

Appendix III: Expenditures in 2011 for the
Emerging Markets Program, Quality Samples
Program, and Technical Assistance for
Specialty Crops Program

Table 10: Program Participants with Largest Expenditures for Technical Assistance for Specialty Crops Program (TASC) in 2011

Dollars in thousands

Participant ranking by expenditure amount		TASC expenditures
1	California Grape & Tree Fruit League	$460
2	Washington Tree Fruit Research Commission	334
3	California Olive Oil Council	252
4	Chapman University	221
5	Bryant Christie	169
6	Florida Department of Citrus	167
7	U.S. Hop Industry Plant Protection Committee	146
8	Indian River Citrus League	139
9	California Table Grape Commission	125
10	Idaho State Department of Agriculture	123
Participants' total expenditures (percentage of all TASC participants' expenditures)		**$2,136 (79%)**
All TASC participants' expenditures		**$2,717**

Source: GAO analysis of USDA data.

Notes:

Twenty-one organizations expended TASC funds in 2011.

Numbers in columns may not sum to totals because of rounding.

Data shown are as of September 25, 2012.

Appendix III: Expenditures in 2011 for the
Emerging Markets Program, Quality Samples
Program, and Technical Assistance for
Specialty Crops Program

Table 11: Countries Where Largest Amounts of Emerging Markets Program (EMP), Quality Samples Program (QSP), and Technical Assistance Specialty Crops Program (TASC) Funds Were Spent in 2011

Dollars in thousands

Country ranking by share of expenditures		Expenditures	Share of total expenditures
EMP			
1	United States	$802	**28%**
2	China	539	**19**
3	Nigeria	293	**10**
4	Burkina	253	**9**
5	Afghanistan	116	**4**
6	South Africa	110	**4**
7	Dominican Republic	83	**3**
8	India	81	**3**
9	Turkey	67	**2**
10	Sri Lanka	58	**2**
Total		**$2,401**	**83%**
QSP			
1	China	$284	**34%**
2	India	75	**9**
3	Thailand	67	**8**
4	Mexico	63	**8**
5	Russia	60	**7**
6	Morocco	38	**5**
7	Philippines	37	**4**
8	South Africa	36	**4**
9	Republic of the Congo	33	**4**
10	Vietnam	26	**3**
Total		**$718**	**86%**
TASC			
1	United States	$2,300	**85%**
2	Australia	125	**5**
3	Germany	84	**3**
4	Japan	83	**3**
5	Mexico	49	**2**
6	Afghanistan	40	**1**
7	India	24	**1**

Appendix III: Expenditures in 2011 for the
Emerging Markets Program, Quality Samples
Program, and Technical Assistance for
Specialty Crops Program

Dollars in thousands

Country ranking by share of expenditures		Expenditures	Share of total expenditures
8	Taiwan	12	.4
Total		**$2,717**	**100%**

Source: GAO analysis of USDA data.

Notes:

TASC funds were expended in eight countries in 2011.

Although the United States does not have diplomatic relations with Taiwan, we have listed it as a separate country because whenever the laws of the United States refer or relate to foreign countries, nations, states, governments, or similar entities, such terms shall include and shall apply to Taiwan.

Numbers in columns may not sum to totals because of rounding.

Data shown are as of September 25, 2012.

Appendix IV: Cost-Benefit Analyses Assert That Several Market Failures Justify FAS Programs

The 2007 study and 2010 update contended that three market failures lead private firms to underinvest in export promotion compared with the socially optimal level. According to the study, these failures therefore justify U.S. government intervention through the U.S. Department of Agriculture market development programs.[1]

- **Uncertain funding.** Because of uncertainty about annual U.S. government allocations of market development funding, private-sector participants tend to develop short-term (i.e., 1 year) plans that do not take into account the long-term effects of market development. For example, market development expenditures for high-value and bulk commodities have a lagged impact of 7 and 3 years, respectively, so that expenditures in a single year accrue benefits over several years. As a result, private-sector participants tend to underfund market development activities relative to the socially optimal level.

- **Spillover effect.** Market development for one commodity may also increase demand for other commodities—a result known as a spillover effect. For example, almond promotions increase grape exports (but not vice versa). Unless such commodities are "co-branded" and marketed together, exporters do not see the spillover effect as a promotion incentive and thus tend to underpromote their own products compared with socially optimal levels.

- **Indirect effect.** Related to the first two sources of market failure, less than optimal amounts of promotion, and therefore of exports, will lead—in what is known as the indirect effect—to less than socially optimal operating levels in other segments of the farm economy and the general economy. To the extent that exports benefit other sectors of the general economy, such as by increasing growers' prices and government tax revenues, there is a compelling public interest in helping firms to develop new export markets for U.S. agricultural commodities.

---

[1]According to the 2007 study, the federal role in agricultural market development is justifiable under two conditions: (1) A market failure leads private firms to under invest in export promotion compared with the socially optimal level. (2) A compelling public interest in export promotion exists that would justify additional private-sector market promotion. A market failure is commonly defined as a situation in which an unregulated competitive market is inefficient, because prices fail to provide proper signals to consumers and producers. In the presence of a market failure, the government can intervene and provide policy through regulation, taxes, or subsidies to bring the market to equilibrium.

Appendix V: Computable General Equilibrium Model

The 2007 cost-benefit analysis that the Foreign Agricultural Service (FAS) commissioned used a computable general equilibrium model, in addition to a market share model and a spillover effect model, to examine the economic impacts of FAS's Market Access Program and the Foreign Market Development Program. A computable general equilibrium model is a mathematical expression where all economic relationships are modeled simultaneously. For example, the price of a good depends on the price of all other input goods, profits, and wages, and vice versa, assuming full employment in the economy. Compared with the market share or spillover effect model, the computable general equilibrium model includes a more comprehensive list of relevant variables while allowing more parameters to vary.[1]

Using this model, the 2007 study found the following key results:

- The FAS program and participant promotion expenditures under the 2002 farm bill present an economic-welfare-to-government-expense ratio of 10.3:1 and an economic-welfare-to-total-expense ratio of 5.2:1. This result translates into an increase in farm cash receipts of $2.2 billion.[2]

- The FAS program and participant promotion expenditures under a hypothetical 2007 farm bill presented a potential economic-welfare-to-government-expense ratio of 8.2:1 and an economic-welfare-to-total-expense ratio of 4.1:1, with a total economic benefit of $740 million. In addition, for the period 2008-2012, farm revenues would equal $256 billion under the hypothetical 2007 farm bill and would change by $2.4 billion and -$4.2 billion under the increasing and eliminating scenarios, respectively.

---

[1]The study used the framework from the global trade analysis project agriculture model.

[2]An economic welfare–expense ratio of x:1 means that the economic welfare increased by x for every dollar spent.

Appendix VI: Comments from the U.S. Department of Agriculture

United States
Department of
Agriculture

Farm and Foreign
Agricultural
Services

Foreign
Agricultural
Service

1400 Independence
Ave, SW
Stop 1001
Washington, DC
20250-1001

Lawrance Evans, Jr.
Director, International Affairs and Trade
United States Government Accountability Office
441 G Street, N.W.
Washington, D.C. 20548

JUL 22 2013

Dear Mr. Evans:

The U.S. Department of Agriculture (USDA) appreciates this opportunity to review and comment on the Government Accountability Office (GAO) draft report entitled "USDA Is Monitoring Market Development Programs as Required but Could Improve Analysis of Impact" (GAO-13-740). We are pleased GAO found that the Foreign Agricultural Service (FAS) has established processes to mitigate risks of duplication among the five market development programs, to monitor participant expenditures, and to assess program results. The Department notes GAO's recommendations that program participants identify the methodologies used to assess results, and that future cost-benefit analyses include industry-specific variables and sensitivity analyses of key assumptions. USDA agrees with these recommendations and will take the following actions to address them.

Emphasize the importance for participants to identify methodologies used to assess results for each performance measure in annual country progress reports

FAS is aware of the importance that every program participant's performance measures include clear and strong methodologies. FAS will highlight that fact at the annual meeting of program participants scheduled to be held this November. FAS also will make the requirement explicit in the program application review process, clarifying that a constraint/performance measure cannot be considered adequate without a methodology identified. Finally, FAS will emphasize the importance in future feedback letters to participants as well.

Ensure that future cost-benefit analyses include industry-specific variables known to have a significant role in determining U.S. market share

FAS will ensure that any Request for Proposal (RFP) to undertake a program-wide cost-benefit analysis encourages vendors to address various approaches in their methodologies, including the additional variables recommended by GAO in this draft report. Vendors responding to the RFP will provide their bid on the study along with their planned methodologies, and FAS will assess the best selection from the proposals submitted, taking into account the considerations that GAO identified.

USDA is an Equal Opportunity Employer

Conduct a sensitivity analysis of the key assumptions that are applied in any economic models used in the cost-benefit analysis

FAS will include a requirement for a sensitivity analysis of key assumptions in any cost-benefit analysis RFP.

We would like to thank the GAO for its review and recommendations regarding the USDA market development programs.

Sincerely,

Phil Karsting
Administrator
Foreign Agricultural Service

Appendix VII: GAO Contacts and Staff Acknowledgments

GAO Contact	Lawrance Evans Jr., (202) 512-4802 or evansl@gao.gov
Staff Acknowledgments	In addition to the individual named above, Christine Broderick (Assistant Director), Pedro Almoguera, Mason Thorpe Calhoun, Howard Cott, Kathryn Crosby, Martin De Alteriis, Justin Fisher, Reid Lowe, Grace Lui, and Vanessa Taylor made significant contributions to this report.

GAO's Mission	The Government Accountability Office, the audit, evaluation, and investigative arm of Congress, exists to support Congress in meeting its constitutional responsibilities and to help improve the performance and accountability of the federal government for the American people. GAO examines the use of public funds; evaluates federal programs and policies; and provides analyses, recommendations, and other assistance to help Congress make informed oversight, policy, and funding decisions. GAO's commitment to good government is reflected in its core values of accountability, integrity, and reliability.
Obtaining Copies of GAO Reports and Testimony	The fastest and easiest way to obtain copies of GAO documents at no cost is through GAO's website (http://www.gao.gov). Each weekday afternoon, GAO posts on its website newly released reports, testimony, and correspondence. To have GAO e-mail you a list of newly posted products, go to http://www.gao.gov and select "E-mail Updates."
Order by Phone	The price of each GAO publication reflects GAO's actual cost of production and distribution and depends on the number of pages in the publication and whether the publication is printed in color or black and white. Pricing and ordering information is posted on GAO's website, http://www.gao.gov/ordering.htm. Place orders by calling (202) 512-6000, toll free (866) 801-7077, or TDD (202) 512-2537. Orders may be paid for using American Express, Discover Card, MasterCard, Visa, check, or money order. Call for additional information.
Connect with GAO	Connect with GAO on Facebook, Flickr, Twitter, and YouTube. Subscribe to our RSS Feeds or E-mail Updates. Listen to our Podcasts. Visit GAO on the web at www.gao.gov.
To Report Fraud, Waste, and Abuse in Federal Programs	Contact: Website: http://www.gao.gov/fraudnet/fraudnet.htm E-mail: fraudnet@gao.gov Automated answering system: (800) 424-5454 or (202) 512-7470
Congressional Relations	Katherine Siggerud, Managing Director, siggerudk@gao.gov, (202) 512-4400, U.S. Government Accountability Office, 441 G Street NW, Room 7125, Washington, DC 20548
Public Affairs	Chuck Young, Managing Director, youngc1@gao.gov, (202) 512-4800 U.S. Government Accountability Office, 441 G Street NW, Room 7149 Washington, DC 20548